D0752645

The Inquisitive Cook

Anne Gardiner and Sue Wilson
with the Exploratorium

An Exploratorium Book

An Owl Book
Henry Holt and Company   New York

Henry Holt and Company, Inc.
Publishers since 1866
115 West 18th Street
New York, New York 10011

Henry Holt® is a registered trademark
of Henry Holt and Company, Inc.

Published in Canada by Fitzhenry & Whiteside Ltd.,
195 Allstate Parkway, Markham, Ontario L3R 4T8.

Library of Congress Cataloging-in-Publication Data
Gardiner, Anne.
    The inquisitive cook / Anne Gardiner and Sue Wilson, with the
Exploratorium.
        p. cm.—(Accidental scientist) (Exploratorium book)
        ISBN 0-8050-4541-4
    I. Wilson, Sue. II. Exploratorium (Organization) III. Title.
IV. Series. V. Series: Exploratorium book.
TX651.G37 1998
641.5—dc21   97-49851
                                                         CIP

Henry Holt Books are available for special promotions
and premiums. For details, contact: Director, Special Markets.

First Edition 1998

Designed by Gary Crounse

Be careful! The experiments in this publication were designed
with safety and success in mind. But even the simplest activity
or most common materials can be harmful when mishandled
or misused.

The Exploratorium® is a registered trademark and service
mark of The Exploratorium.

Printed in the United States of America

All first editions are printed on acid-free paper. ∞

10 9 8 7 6 5 4 3 2

In memory of Dad,
who loved life, his family, and fine food

Contents

Acknowledgments

Writing a book is like making fine stock. Good ingredients are important, but it's the way they work together that results in a full, rich broth. In this project, we've had the great joy of working with an incredibly dynamic team at the Exploratorium. We offer heartfelt thanks to:

Pat Murphy, editor extraordinaire, who stood by patiently—always sampling, sometimes suggesting new ingredients, or more of one and less of another. We've learned a lot from our collaboration and the book is stronger because of her skill.

Kurt Feichtmeir, for launching this project in such fine fashion, and for his continuing interest in how the stock was coming along.

Esther Kutnick, whose drawings liven the text, much as spices and herbs add fresh nuances of flavor, or highlight those already present.

All the other folks at the Exploratorium who helped bring this project to completion.

David Sobel, of Henry Holt and Company, for his enthusiasm, his perceptive questions, and for occasionally pushing us to stir the pot in new ways.

The experts at the following agencies who were generous with their time and knowledge: The Beef Information Centre, Vancouver; The Canadian Sugar Institute, Toronto; The Monell Chemical Senses Center, Philadelphia; Fleischmann's Yeast, San Francisco.

And just as the best stock develops slowly, a book never comes into being without background support.

To our husbands, Don and Dan, and our families: Kathryn, Dave, and Steve; Sara, Meghan, and Kathryn. Like leeks, onions, and shallots, each has contributed, in his or her own way, layer after layer of interest, patience, and encouragement. We love you all.

We send a large bouquet garni to Mum, for making us conscious of fine food and high standards and for teaching us, at a very early age, about the importance of good stock.

—Anne Gardiner and Sue Wilson

Introduction

Welcome to The Accidental Scientist, a series of books created by the Exploratorium to help you discover the science that's part of things you do every day.

In *The Inquisitive Cook,* we investigate the science of muffins and popovers, of sautéing and simmering, of angel food cake and custard. We answer questions that will help you improve your cooking, whether you are a beginning cook or a master chef. Why do mashed potatoes get gooey? Why do you sauté onions before adding tomato sauce? Can you add extra baking powder if you want extra-high muffins? Can curdled hollandaise sauce be saved?

The Inquisitive Cook is filled with experiments that you can try in your own kitchen. Bake muffins and notice what happens when you stir the batter too enthusiastically. Caramelize sugar and observe its chemical changes—while making delicious pralined almonds. Poach apples and discover why you add sugar to applesauce after the apples have cooked, rather than before.

At the Exploratorium, San Francisco's museum of science, art, and human perception, we believe that learning how things work is not only fascinating and fun, but can also expand and enrich your experience of your favorite activities. Knowing why lettuce wilts can help you create the right conditions to keep the leaves crisp. Realizing how ingredients in a bread recipe interact can help you understand why some recipes fail. And understanding the science behind ingredients and techniques can help you improve your cooking.

Be warned: We've found that once you start noticing the science in your kitchen, you may find it difficult to stop. You'll find yourself aware of things that you never paid any attention to before and asking questions that you never thought to ask. Have fun!

Goéry Delacôte
Director
Exploratorium

The Inside Story

All cooks have moments of high drama while working in their kitchens. In our memory banks are Sue's singed eyebrows from bending too close to the Christmas pudding while pouring on the flaming brandy. We laugh at how steep the learning curve is at such times.

We've also learned a lot about cooking in ways that are just as effective, but a tad less theatrical. For instance, Anne finally achieved the perfect cheesecake with carefully thought-out changes to a traditional recipe. Altered in both texture and appearance, the result was high and elegant. No cracks on the surface. A silky interior, cradled in a crushed rusk crust. Just firm enough to hold its shape when sliced. Ambrosia at its finest! Mission accomplished.

But sometimes, learning about cooking involves simply being an astute observer. Have you noticed the tiny happenings as broccoli begins to cook in hot water? As the vegetable's cell walls begin to soften, oxygen tumbles out along the stem in miniature bubbles.

Delicate airy strings, as perfect as transparent jewelry, whirl from freshly cut stem ends. As oxygen leaves, you'll see the broccoli becoming momentarily brighter in color. In fresh broccoli, oxygen stored in the cells camouflages some of its natural green. And that vivid shade differs dramatically from the color broccoli becomes if it endures prolonged cooking. Ah, but we're getting ahead of ourselves; that's another chapter in the story.

What began years ago as simply seeking answers to our own questions has subtly but surely become a quest, and yes, a passion for understanding what happens when we cook.

When a recipe flopped, we didn't just discard it. We wanted to know why the soufflé didn't rise, why some cookies

Knowing why some things work and others don't continues to help us improve recipes and adapt them to our own needs and tastes, often in easy ways.

are soft and others crisp, why red cabbage sometimes turns blue, why you can't just leave the sugar out of a recipe. Such questions soon led us beyond our own cooking backgrounds to research journals, textbooks, and technical experts in the food industry.

We even went so far as to try recipes that didn't make sense (not all recipes are good ones), just to see if they worked—in spite of a peculiar combination of ingredients or an odd method of putting them together. Knowing why some things work and others don't continues to help us improve recipes and adapt them to our own needs and tastes, often in easier ways.

We've learned that cooking often means cajoling ingredients into doing things they don't normally do—such as beating recalcitrant egg whites so they stretch around air bubbles to create the foam for an elegant soufflé. Knowing the best way to create a foam and the factors that affect it makes a big difference to the success of recipes that use beaten egg whites.

In fact, understanding about food can make a difference to something as simple as the add-ons to a hamburger. For example, if you like putting crisp lettuce on your hamburger, it's good to know that small whole leaves of fresh lettuce stay crunchy longer

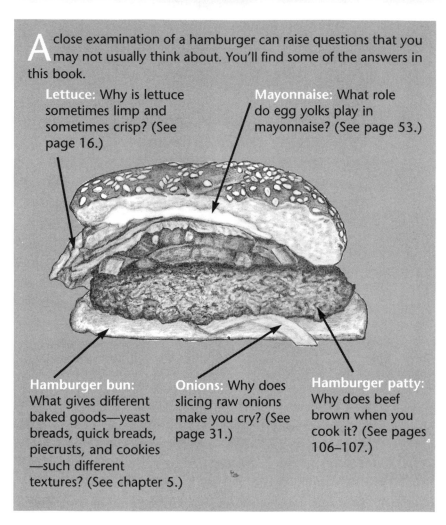

A close examination of a hamburger can raise questions that you may not usually think about. You'll find some of the answers in this book.

Lettuce: Why is lettuce sometimes limp and sometimes crisp? (See page 16.)

Mayonnaise: What role do egg yolks play in mayonnaise? (See page 53.)

Hamburger bun: What gives different baked goods—yeast breads, quick breads, piecrusts, and cookies —such different textures? (See chapter 5.)

Onions: Why does slicing raw onions make you cry? (See page 31.)

Hamburger patty: Why does beef brown when you cook it? (See pages 106–107.)

because their cells are full and taut with moisture. Moisture drains quickly from lettuce cells that have been sliced or chopped. Once those cells are no longer full, their structure collapses. Yet how often do fast-food outlets have tubs of shredded lettuce limply waiting for an order?

As we learned more about common, everyday ingredients, we acquired enormous respect for their characteristics, capabilities, and foibles. We discovered the qualities in flour that contribute to top-notch yeast breads or the most tender pastry. We considered the colors in vegetables—some are stabilized by a little lemon juice, others destroyed. We learned about the difference simmering versus boiling makes to the tenderness of a homey beef stew.

Designing and teaching a course called "The Chemistry of Cooking" gave us license to pursue our questions about food in the academic world and to imbue our students with the same curiosity. We often think back to that very first class in 1983, when we expected to catch the interest of a few keen cooks. Much to our surprise and delight, the class was packed. And more people were standing at the door hoping there might be extra spaces. We quickly discovered that people of all ages, from novice cooks to pros, are curious about how cooking works.

As we teach and write, our students and readers tell us that once they begin asking questions and getting answers, even familiar ingredients become fascinating. "I didn't know I had so much to learn about things I do every day," is a sentiment we often hear.

Learning About Cooking; Thinking About Food

No matter how busy the day, everyone spends time eating. And for many, each day also includes other food-related activities— shopping, preparing meals, storing food, and cleaning up. With food occupying so much of people's lives, it seems strange that many cooks know so little about the inside story of cooking.

After years of wondering why this was so, we feel that it's partly due to the ways that cooking know-how has been passed from one generation to the next. How and when you learn to work with food shapes how you think about it. Before the age of measuring utensils or scales, your ancestors learned to cook by repeating the actions of others and using a "handful" of this, a "pinch" of that. Usually, learning took place at home while helping with the meals, standing alongside one's grandmother, mother, or the cook as she worked in the kitchen. Learning to prepare meals took place through a casual sort of apprenticeship, one in which practice made perfect.

But sometimes people keep on using the cooking methods that they learned as children without ever thinking them through. We've heard an anecdote about a woman following her mother's instructions for cooking a roast. She always cut the roast in half and put it in two pans, since that was the way her mother did it. Some years later, she asked her mother why she had to cook it in two pans. Would cooking it in one pan change the flavor? Her mother replied that she'd always used two pans because she didn't have one that was big enough to hold the entire roast.

Sometimes people keep on using the cooking methods that they learned as children without ever thinking them through.

Today, people still learn to cook by repeating the actions of others, though often in more formal circumstances, such as classrooms or cooking schools. Now, when a beginner can't personally be with an instructor, television cooking shows or cooking videos reinvent the apprenticeship experience in a new form.

In past times, when families scattered, written instructions became increasingly important. Since those instructions didn't show exactly what grandmother's "handful" really looked like, more accurate ways of measuring took the guesswork out of cooking. Written recipes have become the vehicles through which cooks communicate. In essence, they're really formulas phrased in cooking jargon. And while these recipes can't convey a grandmother's loving touch, they work well, for the most part. They stimulate you to use ingredients in new ways. Often, their careful instructions leave little to chance.

But despite all the successes of muffins, biscuits, and sauces, there's a downside to the precision of recipes. When only this aspect of preparing food is emphasized, cooking can become just mechanically following instructions. There's little need to be inquisitive or creative if the cooking process stresses only the steps you must follow.

We still recall vividly teaching a class of novice chefs in a well-respected cooking school some years ago. As we entered the classroom we remarked to the owner, a fine chef, that he was welcome to join us. He refused with the curt comment that, "I teach my students to 'do'... not to think." We beg to differ. Cooking is at its best when it stimulates not only the taste buds, but also one's curiosity. One of the students in that class later quietly expressed the sentiment that if he'd understood the role of gluten earlier, he would have saved a lot of time as he learned to make pastry. We can't help but agree.

New Spin on Food

When most people think about food and science, one of the first things that comes to mind is nutrition. It would be foolish to underestimate the importance of a healthy diet, but highlighting only the nutrients and the number of calories in a day's meals limits the ways you think about food. Today, it's very easy to become accustomed to thinking that what food does for your body is the most important part of eating. But that's not the only way of thinking about science and food.

Much of the information that scientists have found is seldom called to the attention of everyday cooks.

The culinary world owes much of its knowledge about food to the keen minds, remarkable curiosity, and painstaking research of generations of scientists in many diverse fields such as agriculture, chemistry, biology, physics, and food science. Their work has improved not only the quality of our food supply, but also the variety of foods we can now access, and the safety of what we eat. Yet much of the information that scientists have found is seldom called to the attention of everyday cooks, perhaps because cooking developed by modeling the actions of others rather than relying on academic input. So the domain of science has remained apart from the world of cooking—although indirectly its influence has been profound.

We think that the organic food movement helped encourage people to be more curious about food. Diligently searching for the

How foods are grown, harvested, and stored can affect their flavor and other characteristics. Home-grown tomatoes, for example, are usually much tastier than those you buy in the supermarket. Since ripe tomatoes are difficult to ship, most commercially grown tomatoes are picked green, shipped to their destination, then treated with ethylene gas, which stimulates tomatoes to ripen. Ethylene-ripened tomatoes don't develop all the flavor compounds found in vine-ripened fruit.

freshest and most flavorful ingredients meant asking questions—about growing conditions, varieties, harvesting, transport, and storage. While intuition and aesthetics still played a part in selecting ingredients, new types of knowledge were also needed. What did experts in a variety of fields have to say? A new facet of food's relationship to science began trickling down to the home kitchen.

A good cook is also highly cognizant of creating flavors. After all, one of the compelling reasons for cooking is to make food tastier. Heating, browning, fermenting, and often merely mixing liquids and dry ingredients together can set in motion physical and chemical changes that create new flavors and aromas. So roasted vegetables provide a whole different eating experience than the same vegetables boiled. And bread with a well-browned crust is more flavorful than a loaf that's barely colored.

We believe that if you use this book as your companion in the kitchen along with your favorite recipes, you will find that understanding the hows and whys of cooking is empowering. Knowing the role of ingredients and the logic of techniques gives you an edge for making not only wise changes, but creative ones as well. And one success will lead to many others.

As you work with food, it's comforting to realize that the finest food isn't necessarily the fanciest. Much of the best cooking rests on doing the common, uncommonly well. The following chapters are designed to spark your curiosity about the ingredients you may use every day. And it could be that, just like us, you too become hooked on a new dimension of cooking.

We believe that if you use this book as your companion in the kitchen along with your favorite recipes, you will find that understanding the hows and whys of cooking is empowering.

From Roots to Fruits

S ue's
old wooden
salad bowl provides a
rough measure of how many more
salads her family is eating now than they were a decade ago.
Originally they considered this bowl so large that it was only
brought out for parties. Now it's used regularly, as hearty salads
are frequently a main course at family dinners.

Sue's experience is probably typical of many people's changing
food patterns. It's not just more salads. Many of us are including an
increasing number of other fruits and vegetables in our meals. At
the same time, the variety and the quality of fresh produce is
steadily improving. In many markets, the produce is not only beautiful to look at (the crinkled surface of a cut red cabbage is as intricate as an etching), but also a pleasure to work with in the kitchen.

For us, much of the appeal of working with fruits and vegetables lies in their diversity. It's like being bestowed with a palette that has not only exceptional colors, but also extraordinary textures and flavors—from mellow to blistering. But it takes some know-how to work effectively with such magical possibilities. Handling greens poorly turns their bright colors muddy or olive. The flavors of some vegetables become stronger, even unpleasant, if they are cooked too long. Others mellow during cooking. Understanding the factors that affect fresh produce allows you to make fruits and vegetables either a striking focus or subtle background players in your meals.

The Parts We Eat

In times past, new vegetables and fruits were viewed with great suspicion. Many a sermon was preached about the imprudence of sampling these dicey, unknown foods. Even the potato was once thought to be poisonous, to provoke uncontrollable lust, and to cause insanity. And references to the erotic avocado? Spare us such folly! Thank goodness later generations of cooks were bold enough to sample previously unknown foods.

Even the potato was once thought to be poisonous, to provoke uncontrollable lust, and to cause insanity.

To understand vegetables, you need to consider how they grow. Once fruits and vegetables are picked, they no longer have access to their food and water supply, yet their cells continue their metabolic processes as if they were still growing. This presents a challenge, because how long fruits and vegetables keep has a lot to do with how you store them. Different parts of the plant understandably have different storage requirements.

A brief look at the ways plants function before they reach the nimble fingers of a cook helps you glimpse the uniqueness of the various roots, leaves, fruits, and seeds that you include in your meals.

Underground Vegetables

Carrots, parsnips, jicama, beets, sweet potatoes, and radishes are all the roots of plants. Those vegetables with single large roots are known as taproots. When you pull a carrot from the garden, it's quickly obvious that one function of a root is to anchor the plant in the ground. The primary function of root systems, however, is to absorb nutrients and water from the soil. Tiny root hairs absorb water and nutrients, while the taproot itself is dedicated to storing extra food as a kind of underground depot.

Next time you slice a carrot, take a close look at the cross section. There's a dark orange center surrounded by paler orange. Look closely and you'll see lines radiating from the core. If you slice the carrot lengthwise, you can see that the dark material in the center runs the length of the carrot. The dark orange center, the central cylinder, contains tubes that carry water up from the roots to the

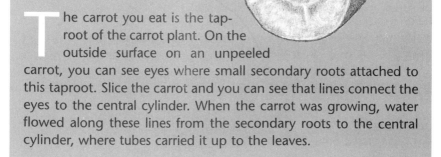

The carrot you eat is the taproot of the carrot plant. On the outside surface on an unpeeled carrot, you can see eyes where small secondary roots attached to this taproot. Slice the carrot and you can see that lines connect the eyes to the central cylinder. When the carrot was growing, water flowed along these lines from the secondary roots to the central cylinder, where tubes carried it up to the leaves.

leaves and tubes that carry food from the leaves back to the tip of the root. The paler orange, called the cortex, is where the carrot stores food. The lines that go to the central cylinder through the cortex are paths where water travels from secondary roots to the central cylinder. Other taproots employ variations on this theme to move their water and sugars.

Though potatoes and onions also grow underground, neither are considered true roots. Potatoes are technically tubers, swollen underground stems, while onions are considered bulbs, below-ground storage systems at the base of the plant's leaves. All these underground vegetables are storage systems, hidden so that predators will pass them by.

It used to be that only folks who had their own gardens could harvest immature underground vegetables. Why uproot these vegetables before they reach their full growth? Because that's when their sugar content is highest and their texture is most tender. Tiny nugget potatoes, baby fingerling carrots, and button beets are now available in more abundance as growers have realized that cooks prize these early season delights. These vegetables are best cooked as soon as possible after picking. As they're stored, their sugar content dissipates. They quickly lose that "just-picked" appeal.

These vegetables are best cooked as soon as possible after picking. As they're stored, their sugar content dissipates. They quickly lose that "just-picked" appeal.

Generally, underground vegetables are less sweet near the end of the growing season. Much of their sugar has been converted to starch as the vegetable matures. However, carrots, parsnips, and even turnips may increase in sweetness if they are left in the ground during cold weather. One theory suggests that the increase in sugar acts as a natural antifreeze to protect some root vegetables from the cold.

Though potatoes are also underground vegetables, their starch turns back to sugar at temperatures below 45°F (7°C), and a sugary potato has an odd flavor. If potatoes are stored at too low a temperature, their sugars also react with amino acids. This gives a double browning reaction in cooking—one from the hot fat and high temperature, the other from sugar and amino acids. Used to make French fries, these potatoes will brown too deeply during frying. Don't store potatoes in the refrigerator. A cool, dark area is best—50°F (10°C) is optimal. If potatoes have been inadvertently refrigerated, leave them out at room temperature for a few days before cooking, and the sugar will convert back to starch again.

While new potatoes are best used within a week after harvest, mature potatoes will keep up to two months. But don't be tempted to store onions right beside the potatoes (a common mistake). Onions give off gases that make potatoes deteriorate quickly—and vice versa.

Root crops were once stored in outside pits or root houses. Now they're generally kept more conveniently in a cool spot, preferably where the humidity is high. When buying root vegetables to store, be sure to choose unblemished ones, as spoilage begins in bruised parts or areas where the skin is broken.

Leaves

Because green plants are living things that have the ability to manufacture their own food, they place some fascinating param-

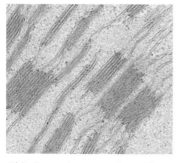

eters on the ways you use them in cooking. The food manufacturing centers of plants are their leaves. When you look at a plant, notice how the arrangement of leaves around the stem is often staggered, so that the higher leaves don't shadow the lower leaves. And most leaves have a large surface area in proportion to their thickness so they can capture as much sunlight as possible.

This is a close-up of a chloro-plast, a microscopic body inside a leaf cell. Within the chloro-plast, you can see stacks of sacs filled with chlorophyll, the pig-ment that gives green plants their color.

Each leaf uses energy from sunlight to manufacture carbohydrates and sugars, which the plant uses as food. In this process, plants consume carbon dioxide and release oxygen into the atmosphere, a boon to us oxygen breathers.

This process is called *photosynthesis*—an intricate interplay between water, carbon dioxide, and chlorophyll, the leaf cells' green pigment. Most of the water that a plant requires travels up to the leaves from the root system, though a small amount is absorbed through the leaves themselves. Air passes in and out through tiny openings in the leaves and stems. Chlorophyll is located in microscopic disks called *chloroplasts* found in the leaf cells.

Chlorophyll traps the energy from sunlight. The plant uses this energy to split water molecules into hydrogen and oxygen atoms and manufacture a carbohydrate, initially a simple sugar. As plants mature, some of this sugar is turned to starch (a storable form of carbohydrate), which provides the plant with a food supply for those cold, dark months when there is too little sunlight for photosynthesis.

Cook's Query

What's the purpose of the crisper in your fridge?

When greens hold water inside their cells they stay crisp. The challenge of keeping produce fresh means maintaining the humidity of the environment at a level close to that of the produce so that the greens don't lose water to the surrounding air. The crisping compartments of your refrigerator offer a confined, moist environment. You may still find that small pieces of fruits or vegetables dehydrate even when placed in the crisper. That's because much of their water evaporates to saturate the empty space around them with water vapor. When you put washed greens in a lightly closed plastic bag, you create a small area of high humidity inside the crisper, keeping your greens fresh.

During the growing season, sugar is also converted to the amino acids that make up both chlorophyll, plant enzymes, and other proteins. To manufacture amino acids, plants also need minerals—nitrogen, sulfur, and phosphorus—which the roots absorb as mineral salts. These ingenious processes of nature are at their peak from spring to fall.

Storing Fresh Greens

Most of the leaves you eat fresh are called simply "greens," or when different varieties of young tender leaves are mixed together, "mesclun." And there are many from which to choose, ranging from spinach to arugula, mizuna, and watercress. When greens are just picked, their cells are plump with water. But on hot days or as they sit in market bins, water soon evaporates from their expansive, delicate surfaces and the green leaves wilt. If leaves are crushed or bruised, they become even more fragile. Keeping greens crunchy and crisp means encouraging them to hold water rather than letting it evaporate.

The walls of plant cells, like gatekeepers, are fussy about what passes through. Water and dissolved gases or minerals can travel freely from one side of a cell wall to the other. But all the other cell contents, such as plant sugars, proteins, organic acids, and most coloring pigments, stay within each cell.

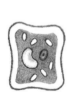

When water evaporates from a leaf, all the substances that can't pass through the membrane remain inside each cell and become increasingly concentrated. Low on water, the cell sags like a balloon losing air. Multiply one deflated cell by millions and it's easy to see how a fragile leaf quickly becomes limp.

A cell in a lettuce leaf surrounded by dry air (left) loses water and sags, leaving the leaf limp and wilted. Plunge that leaf into cool water (right), and water flows back through the cell wall, filling the cell so that the leaf is crisp.

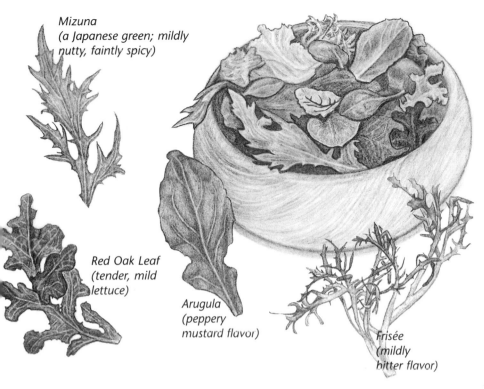

Mizuna
(a Japanese green; mildly nutty, faintly spicy)

Red Oak Leaf
(tender, mild lettuce)

Arugula
(peppery mustard flavor)

Frisée
(mildly bitter flavor)

Mesclun, or salad mix, began as a regional specialty in southern France, but can now be found in many supermarkets. The mixture varies, but often includes the greens pictured here. To keep mesclun crisp, store it in a moist environment (see page 15).

To make a wilting leaf crisp, you need to give those sagging cells a chance to replenish their water supply. If you plunge limp greens into cool water, the water will flow through the cell walls to dilute the contents of the cells. When you do this, you are involved, whether you know it or not, in the business of controlling osmosis. In this situation, *osmosis* refers to the tendency of water to move through the cell membrane until the pressure exerted by the water is the same on both sides of the cell wall.

Because limp cells have lower water pressure than normal and a high concentration of salts and other substances, water moves into the sagging cell. As sagging cells inflate, they exert pressure on the cell walls until a balance in both pressure and concentration is restored. Gradually, each leaf becomes lively and crisp.

FROM ROOTS TO FRUITS

If you wash greens before storing them, sometimes large beads of water remain on the leaves. You don't want to store greens in this state since the moisture encourages bacterial growth, which causes the greens to spoil quickly. Some cooks consider vegetable spinners to be a boon for removing extra moisture from freshly washed produce. Others prefer to wash, drain, and loosely wrap greens in tea towels or paper towels, and then place them in plastic bags in the refrigerator. Within several hours, they are crisp, perfect for eating, and they keep surprisingly well.

See for Yourself
Stewing or poaching?

Have you ever wondered why you were taught to add the sugar to the applesauce after the apples have cooked? Try adding it sooner and see what happens.

Peel, core, and slice cooking apples into a saucepan. Add water one-third of the way up the apples. Bring to a simmer, sweeten— 1 cup (250 ml) sugar per 3 cups (750 ml) water—immediately, and cook until the apples are tender when pierced with a knife.

You'll notice that apples won't mush in a sugar syrup. Instead, the apple slices retain their shape because the concentration of the sugar syrup is similar to the fruit's. If sugar is added to apples as they cook, the apples are actually poaching rather than stewing.

Try it again, but this time add the sugar after the apples are cooked. Watch them break down as water moves into the fruit tissue to dilute the apple's natural sugars. Eventually, the heat-softened cells burst from the pressure of the extra water, creating a mushy texture. Then sweeten to taste. This is not an esoteric exercise, because you've just made applesauce. But you've also been playing with the principles of osmosis by using sugar to control the movement of water in and out of the cells of an apple.

Fruits

According to botanists, fruits are the seed-bearing parts of plants. Such restrained terminology gives little hint of the spectacular variety of fruits that fall under this definition! Some fruits, such as cherries and apricots, have one large seed while others, such as grapes and oranges, contain several seeds. Each segment of a blackberry is a seed. Squash, cucumbers, green beans, eggplants, okra, and tomatoes are really fruits because they contain seeds.

Most fruits have bright colors, appealing aromas, and eye-catching shapes that entice you to pick them and carry their seeds away to new beginnings, far from the competition of the parent plant.

Anne remembers that, as a child, she had the pleasure each summer of going to our orchard in the Okanagan Valley and picking a perfect peach, twisting the fruit gently from a low branch. The rosy blush of the peach's skin was softened by a pale fuzz. Plump and full, it felt warm from the sun. Each peach was so juicy, she had to lean over while eating as peach juice dripped from her hands and chin. The fruit's tree-ripened flavor was something she still recalls vividly, years later.

How lucky she was to grow up believing that all peaches tasted like that, and what a shock it was to find they didn't. Using a process called *chromatography,* scientists can determine what chemical compounds a food contains, producing a display called a *chromatogram.* In chromatograms, showing the flavor-producing compounds of a tree-ripened peach and an artificially ripened one (page 20), the differences are striking. The tree-ripened fruit has about twice as many different volatile flavor-producing compounds—and much, much more of each compound.

Like Anne's peach, most fruits are best when they're allowed to ripen before being picked. There are exceptions to every rule, of course, and a few fruits, such as bananas and pears, are better picked slightly green, and allowed to ripen off the tree.

As fruits ripen, their sugars accumulate, aromatic compounds form, and the pectin that cements their cells together changes to a more soluble form, so their texture softens. Harvesting fruit at its peak is ideal but often difficult today, when orchards and markets

Tree-ripened peach

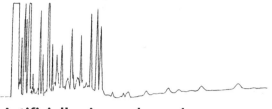

Artificially ripened peach

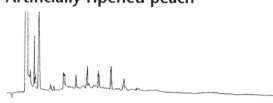

Science confirms what your taste buds tell you. Each spike in these chromatograms represents a different flavor compound. You can see that an artificially ripened peach has fewer flavor compounds and less of each compound than a tree-ripened peach.

may be thousands of miles apart. Modern agriculture has had a profound (and sometimes unwelcome) impact on food flavor. For the most part, fruits and vegetables are grown for yield and ease in transportation, rather than for optimal production of flavor.

Fresh fruits do not generally keep well. As the ripening process continues in the picked fruit, textures become mushy and flavors deteriorate. With many fresh fruits, refrigeration is the key to keeping them longer, for as with vegetables, the enzymes that cause ripening work more slowly in the cold.

Some produce of tropical origin, however, is subject to injury if it's stored at temperatures below 50°F (10°C). So cucumbers, tomatoes, eggplants, bananas, snap beans, peppers, winter squash, and sweet potatoes are best stored at cool, but not cold, temperatures.

Holding Browns at Bay

You've probably noticed that raw fruits and vegetables turn brown sometimes after you peel and slice them. That happens when compounds called *phenols* react with oxygen in the presence of plant enzymes to form brown pigments or *melanins*. You don't even notice this reaction when it contributes (in minor ways) to the

Cook's Queries
What causes a bruise on an apple?

When you accidentally knock an apple off your kitchen counter, it starts to discolor at the spot where it hit the floor. Even though the skin isn't broken, the impact damages the cells and squashes the surrounding air spaces. As the air reacts with the phenolic compounds and enzymes found in the cells, the apple turns brown where the damage has occurred. This is the under-the-skin browning that we commonly call a bruise.

When is a fruit a vegetable?

Often you use the fruit of a plant as a vegetable. When you do that, is it then a fruit? Or a vegetable? For the tomato, this question resulted in a legal case that reached the United States Supreme Court in 1893. At that time, a tariff act applied to imported vegetables. The focus of this case was a load of tomatoes imported from the West Indies to New York. The importer argued that since tomatoes were botanically fruit, they should be exempt from import duty. Justice Horace Gray ruled that tomatoes were vegetables, based on the fact that they were served with the principle part of dinner, while most fruits were used as desserts. His decision established customary use and common language as more important than anatomy. The humble tomato set a precedent. Produce such as squash, cucumbers, and peppers are legally vegetables, though botanically speaking, they are fruits.

natural coloring of raisins, prunes, dates, and figs. Understandably, however, you object when a tinge of brown shadows the pristine white surface of a perfect pear soon after you slice it. Likewise, it's annoying when bananas, peaches, apricots, avocados, apples, and even some potatoes turn brown.

No browning takes place when susceptible produce is left whole, because enzymes and phenolic compounds are segregated by their cell structures and protected from the air by skin. It isn't until you cut or bite or peel a piece of fruit that the cell walls are damaged, throwing together the compounds responsible for browning.

Browning isn't harmful, but you can control it in several simple ways that either inhibit the enzymes or keep oxygen away. If you're peeling a large number of potatoes, cover them with water to keep oxygen away from the exposed surfaces, keeping browning at bay until cooking stops the enzyme activity. Refrigerating cut fruits helps prevent browning, because enzymes work more slowly at cool temperatures.

Poaching or blanching also destroys these enzymes so they can no longer trigger browning. In addition, the sugar in a poaching syrup provides a barrier to air. Increasing the acidity of the surroundings also retards enzyme activity. This is the basis of the action of ascorbic acid and the fruit preservative products that are sold as aids to canning. Ascorbic acid (aka vitamin C), an antioxidant, combines with oxygen before the air has a chance to reach the phenols responsible for browning. For small amounts of fruit, a sprinkling of lemon juice works just fine.

Seeds

When you enjoy fresh green peas, sweet corn, and green beans, you're eating immature seeds. Sweet corn held for even an hour or two after picking deteriorates in quality. So the old adage about "running to the cooking pot with freshly picked corn" is based on reliable folk wisdom. Garden peas lose their sweetness even faster. If it's impossible to eat them right away, these vegetables should be cooled promptly after picking and stored in the refrigerator, since the conversion of sugar to starch takes place more slowly at cool temperatures. As in many other vegetables, the sugar in peas and beans is replaced by starch as the growing season continues. Once peas and beans are fully mature, they are often dried and then they are classified as starchy vegetables, not green vegetables.

Next time you buy green beans, try sampling one bean before cooking, and another after. Thinking about the differences in flavor, appearance, and texture helps you gain a greater respect for the tremendous impact of heat and moisture on fruits and vegetables.

Since heat stops the cell activities in fruits and vegetables, a new set of factors influences these foods once cooking begins. The question then becomes: How can you control changes in taste, look, and feel as fruits and vegetables cook?

Quick Tips for Cooking the Mustards

1 Use enough water to cover the vegetable.

2 Have water already boiling before the vegetable is added.

3 Use an open pan, or keep the lid ajar.

4 Cook quickly until just tender crisp.

Flavor and Odor

It's interesting that one's perception of flavor evolves from how something smells as well as how it tastes. In this section, we look closely at two strong-natured vegetable families—cabbage and garlic. Each has a unique character that must be respected in cooking.

The mustard family (genus Brassica) becomes stronger in flavor and odor the longer it's cooked. Others in this family include broccoli, Brussels sprouts, cauliflower, kale, kohlrabi, rutabaga, and turnip.

Recall the pervasive odor of overcooked cabbage as it sulks across the kitchen. It's a member of the mustard family (genus *Brassica*) that becomes stronger in flavor and odor the longer it's cooked. Others in this family include broccoli, Brussels sprouts, cauliflower, kale, kohlrabi, rutabaga, and turnip.

The pungent qualities of these vegetables come from several sulfur-containing compounds, which are by-products of *isothiocyanates,* or mustard oils. In more powerful form, these compounds add the zip to commercial mustards and bottled horseradish. But when cabbage is poorly cooked, these compounds can become quite disagreeable.

As cabbage cooks, mustard oil compounds break down and release hydrogen sulfide, which smells like rotten eggs. The amount of hydrogen sulfide produced in boiled cabbage doubles after five to seven minutes of cooking. Ammonia, methyl sulfide, and various compounds called *mercaptans* also contribute to the unwelcome odor and stronger flavors. You should, therefore, cook this family of vegetables in ways that minimize their assertive character.

In contrast, the lily family (genus *Allium*) mellows as it cooks. Garlic is its most pungent member, but others in this family are onions, chives, and shallots.

See for Yourself
Roasting garlic

When you roast garlic, use the whole head. Peel away the papery outer covering, but leave each clove, covered by its skin, still firmly attached to the base. Lightly brush the surface of the garlic with olive oil and place in a baking dish. Add 3 tablespoons (50 ml) butter and 3 tablespoons (50 ml) chicken stock. Bake for one hour at 350°F (180°C), basting frequently. Just before serving, sprinkle with coarse salt.

Pinch each clove and it pops right out of its skin. Serve alongside roasted meat, or as a hot appetizer with melted Brie, crusty fresh bread, and a glass of wine. Notice how gentle and delicately aromatic garlic becomes, once tamed by cooking.

Inside the cells of each clove of garlic, there's an odorless molecule called *alliin*. In the spaces between the cells, there's an enzyme called *alliinase*. Cutting a garlic clove throws the two together, creating a series of reactions that result in the familiar intense flavor and odor. So, the more finely you mince or chop fresh garlic, the greater the contact, and the stronger the flavor.

Members of the lily family can be the star of the show if you choose. But they're equally capable of mellowing so their influence is subtle. To bring out this more affable side, bake them slowly, or cook them in lots of water, and allow their pungent compounds to evaporate.

When cooked whole, garlic mellows as its odoriferous molecules are broken down by heat. Recipes for Forty-Clove Garlic Chicken are not as outrageous as they sound because they use whole cloves, which keep alliin and alliinase quite separate until the cell walls soften. By then alliinase doesn't react with the alliin.

Cook's Query
What causes gooey mashed potatoes?

I f you cook starchy potatoes in too much water for too long, or if
you beat them too vigorously after they're cooked, their starch
granules rupture, spilling out trapped water and starch and giving them a pasty, unpleasant texture.

Texture

Old recipe books make little reference to using raw vegetables,
and those that were cooked were boiled so long they must have
practically disintegrated. We've seen instructions that suggest boiling peas gently for 20 to 40 minutes, potatoes for 40 to 60 minutes,
and fresh corn from 15 minutes to half an hour. It's no wonder
many of our ancestors grew up disliking vegetables.

As vegetables cook, their supporting tissues soften, and water
diffuses from their cells. In addition, the chemical compounds that
cement the cell walls together change character so the tissues soften.

It's best to cook most vegetables just to the tender crisp stage.
But a number of factors—such as the cooking method and the
variety, age, and size of the vegetable—affect the number of minutes it takes to reach *your* preferred level of doneness.

In contrast to most vegetables, those of a starchy nature absorb
water as they cook. So baking is often the cooking method
of choice for starchy vegetables because it allows time for starch
granules to swell as they absorb the moisture held inside by the
skin. As the granules expand in the heat, the texture of baking
potatoes (these varieties are higher in starch than waxy potatoes,
or young ones) and squash becomes lighter.

Keeping Colors, Especially Green

Open a can of green chili peppers, and you'll see the devastating consequences of heat and plant acids on green pigments—now drab gray-green! Yes, chlorophyll is volatile—though the process of canning is admittedly one of extreme circumstances.

Heat decomposes chlorophyll. So the longer a green vegetable cooks, the more the nature of its chlorophyll changes. Picture the vivid green of just-cooked broccoli and the muddy olive shade it becomes if cooking continues. There's no doubt that cooking green vegetables as quickly as possible lessens the damage. Using tin or iron cooking pans also changes the color of chlorophyll to a dull brown as these metals alter chlorophyll's molecular configuration.

Chlorophyll is equally touchy about acids. Not only the acids that you add in cooking (like lemon juice), but also the plant acids within the vegetables themselves that escape as the tissues soften in cooking. Leaving the lid ajar on the saucepan for the first few minutes allows some of the volatile acids to escape, diminishing their

Cook's Query

Why do recipes tell you to sauté onions separately, even in a dish that requires further cooking?

Sautéing softens onions so they meld smoothly into a soup or a sauce. This is particularly important if the next step is to combine them with acidic ingredients, like tomatoes or wine. If onions are not softened first, acids in the other ingredients will keep them in firm and distinct pieces.

If you're including onions in a dish such as scalloped potatoes, sautéing the onions lets some of their acids evaporate so there are fewer available to curdle the milk in the sauce.

What's pH?

The acidity of fruits, vegetables, and other ingredients can be measured using a scale called pH, which ranges from 1 to 14. Pure water, which is neither an acid nor a base, is neutral, sitting right in the middle of the scale, with a pH of 7. Acidic fruits and vegetables, such as lemons and tomatoes, have a pH of less than 7. As their pH value drops closer to 0, foods are increasingly acidic.

Foods like egg white and baking soda, with a pH greater than 7, are bases, or alkaline. As their pH value increases, so does the degree of alkalinity.

Note that most foods you eat are acidic. Even bland vegetables, such as potatoes, are slightly on the acid side.

The effect of acids and bases is often unrecognized. They are indeed hidden partners in cooking, because they are capable of exerting a strong influence on color, texture, and flavor.

effect on the chlorophyll. Keeping cooking to a minimum also limits chlorophyll's exposure to acids.

Take care to squeeze lemon juice onto pan-wilted spinach just before serving. If you do it earlier, the acid has time to react with the chlorophyll, turning the spinach an ugly olive color.

Fast methods of cooking, such as microwaving and stir-frying, allow minimal contact between acids and chlorophyll so color is affected very little. The natural greens of the finished vegetables make these methods appealing.

Not all of nature's colors are as touchy as chlorophyll. *Carotenoids*, which are responsible for the yellows, oranges, and red-oranges in fruits and vegetables, are very sturdy pigments. The colors of carrots, corn, squash, sweet potatoes, and red peppers change only slightly whether you braise with moisture or bake them in dry heat. A tomato will collapse as it's roasted, but its red-orange color holds. The stability of their colors means these vegetables can often be prepared ahead of time, a boon to a busy cook.

Acidity of Fruits and Vegetables
(and a few other interesting items)

I t's helpful to know when you're cooking with acidic ingredients, for then you can anticipate what their effects might be. The number at the left tells you the pH of each item. The lower the number, the more acidic the food.

pH	Item
2.0–2.4	Limes, lemons
2.0–4.0	Ginger ale
2.4–3.4	Vinegar
2.8–3.8	Wines
2.9–3.2	Rhubarb
3.0–3.3	Grapefruit
3.4	Strawberries
3.5	Peaches
3.8	Sweet cherries
3.9	Pears
4.0–4.6	Tomatoes
4.0–5.0	Beer
5.0	Pumpkin, carrots
5.2	Turnips, cabbage, squash
5.3	Parsnips, beets
5.4	Sweet potatoes
5.0–5.4	Molasses
5.5	Spinach
5.6	Asparagus, cauliflower
6.1	Potatoes
6.2	Peas
6.3	Corn
7.0–8.5	Crackers
8.0–8.4	Sea water
8.4	Baking soda

Red, blue, and purple foods hold a special fascination because their colors slide from reds into blues according to how they're treated. These shades are due to *anthocyanin* pigments, and include red grapes, apples, cherries, red cabbage, and most berries. Since these pigments are water soluble, their color leaches into cooking water so you can make a rich burgundy blackberry sauce rather than one in which berries are bathed in a thick, clear liquid. Certain minerals also react with these pigments to push them into the blue tones, which you may have noticed if you've cooked red cabbage in a cast iron pan.

Acids prevent red tones from slipping to blues. It's no accident that recipes for red cabbage include vinegar, and berry sauces are finished with a dash of lemon. Even borscht, colored by related pigments, called *betalains,* often contains both lemon and tomato juice to hold the reds in beets and chase away their blues.

The final group of pigments, the *anthoxanthins,* spend much of their lives being invisible. They make their presence known when vegetables are cooked in highly alkaline water. Then onions, cauliflower, turnips, and white cabbage show their secret colors—creams and yellows. If yellowing is a problem where you live, add a little lemon juice, vinegar, or cream of tartar to make the cooking water more acidic.

The secret to cooking the incredibly diverse world of plants lies in learning about their unique qualities—and handling them accordingly. Don't give up if they're not quite what you expect. Try them again. Often the same vegetable or fruit, handled differently, presents a new personality. We think kids are refreshingly honest when they comment, "Well, I don't like parsnips...but I do like these!" (parsnips baked in the oven with an orange juice/brown sugar glaze).

Consider vegetables and fruits to be special gifts to enjoy and use in abundance.

Culinary Curiosities

Why do raw onions make you cry?

It's curious how an onion has no odor until it's cut. Then, wow! It can be a real tearjerker. When you slice an onion, you damage the cell walls, throwing together amino acids (which contain sulfur) and enzymes that trigger chemical reactions. When they come in contact, volatile sulfur-containing compounds form and become airborne. These compounds irritate your eyes and make you cry. The irritating compounds are water soluble, and the flowing tears help dissipate them. When you cook chopped onions, these unstable compounds break down. In nature, these potent compounds deter predators, a sort of chemical alarm system that has helped onions and other members of the lily family survive for thousands of years.

If you dislike the tears that come with peeling onions, try holding the onion under cold running water to carry away sulfur compounds as you peel it. Chilling onions before peeling also helps.

How do legumes add nutrients to the soil?

All plants known as legumes—including peas, beans, and lentils—have a special relationship with unique nitrogen-fixing

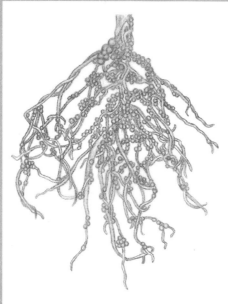

bacteria. When the root system of a legume comes in contact with the bacteria known as *Rhizobium leguminosarum,* in rich, well-aerated soil, the roots build small nodules around the bacteria. Soon tiny capsules of bacteria are interspersed along the roots. The tight covering keeps oxygen away, as these bacteria work best in an anaerobic environment.

Once established, the bacteria begin extracting nitrogen from the air, and converting it to the mineral nitrate. Nitrogen is a plant's most important nutrient, but it can only be used in mineral form because plants can't extract it from the atmosphere. In turn, legumes provide sugars to the bacteria so they can go about their business efficiently. This unusual biological dependency, known as *symbiosis,* benefits both the bacteria and the plants.

How does this ingenious relationship benefit cooking? It builds stronger plants, which in turn yield larger, healthier crops. When the roots of legumes decompose, their nitrates are released to neighboring nonleguminous plants. So, the soil, the plants, and those of us who enjoy legumes are all winners.

Why do apples float?

Luckily for ghosts and goblins who bob for apples on Halloween, 20 to 25 percent of an apple's volume is air—much more than in most fruits. The cells in apple tissue fit imperfectly together. Air sits in the spaces between the cells, not only making apples buoyant, but making a just-picked apple "crack" as you take that first bite.

This photo of the skin and flesh of an apple, magnified to about 120 times its actual size, reveals air pockets between the cells that make up the apple's flesh.

What puts the pop in popcorn?

The key to popping corn is a moisture level of between 11 and 14 percent and a strong, airtight casing. Varieties are carefully engineered to create these crucial factors. Then the kernels are sealed in airtight packages.

When you heat popping kernels, their tiny starch granules swell with moisture, but they're trapped inside the popcorn's hard shell. As the temperature inside the kernel rises beyond the boiling point, water vaporizes and turns to steam. In gaseous form, steam occupies more space than water, so each kernel becomes a tiny pressure cooker. When the pressure gets too great for the kernel's tough overcoat, it explodes and the starch granules instantly expand into a light and fluffy mass.

What about those annoying unpopped kernels left in the bottom of the bowl? Those stubborn kernels present great challenges to popcorn scientists! Due to improper storage, growing conditions, or even the location of the kernel on the cob, their moisture content is usually lower than that of the kernels that popped. Without sufficient moisture, these kernels are unable to muster enough pressure to pop.

The Astonishing Egg

3

I t's not often in life we have the privilege of handling a master-piece of ingenuity. But we do it without thinking when we cook with one of nature's most brilliant creations—the unassuming but extraordinary egg.

For nature's purposes, an egg, once fertilized, is a self-sufficient capsule ready to support the next generation. From a culinary perspective, an egg is a tidy premeasured little sphere of good food value at reasonable cost. We know even before cracking the shell that a large egg is always at least 2 ounces or almost 4 tablespoons (60 ml) of water and protein, vitamins and minerals.

There aren't many foods in which the components are so distinct that sometimes we use one portion and other times the remaining portion. But that's an egg for you.

Eggs are incredibly versatile. Cooked alone, they couldn't be simpler. Combined with other ingredients, eggs become binders, thickeners, clarifiers, emulsifiers, leavens, and structure builders.

Protein is usually the focus of the egg's roles in cooking because proteins can be coddled, stiffened, stretched, and set. Left undisturbed, egg proteins are solitary molecules, made of chains of amino acids, curled into spheres. When cajoled by heating or beating, however, their demeanor changes dramatically. It's as if a reluctant guest is finally convinced to join in the fun and becomes the life of the party. First the proteins unfold, exposing their bonding sites. Then, as they are jostled, they begin to form links with other protein molecules, even-

Left undisturbed, egg proteins are solitary molecules, made of chains of amino acids, curled into spheres. When cajoled by heating or beating, however, their demeanor changes dramatically.

tually creating a three-dimensional network. As heating or beating continues, the links increase and become stronger until the protein sets or coagulates.

The Inner Egg

The next time you break open an egg, look carefully, and you'll see more than simply a yolk and a white. It's really a marvel in design.

First the *chalazae* (pronounced ka-LAY-zee), those tiny white ropes on either side of the yolk, are really twisted cords of dense egg white. Like little anchors, they attach the yolk's casing to the membrane lining the eggshell. Their job is to hold the yolk in the center of the egg, yet still allow it to revolve inside the shell. Chalazae are edible and are seldom removed in cooking. For an ultrasmooth custard, however, strain the egg mixture through a sieve to catch the chalazae before cooking.

Anatomy of an Egg

Chalazae—ropes of egg white that anchor the yolk in the center of the egg. The more prominent they are, the fresher the egg.

Egg white—proteins coagulate at a lower temperature than the proteins in the yolk.

Yolk—a source of lecithin, an effective emulsifier.

Germ spot—the point at which the sperm would enter the egg to fertilize it.

Air space—gets larger as an egg ages.

Clinging tightly inside the shell are two transparent protein membranes that provide efficient defense against bacterial invasion. To the naked eye, it may look like there's just one membrane. But maybe you've noticed the air space that's at the fat end of the egg, the one that often makes a crater in the end of a hard-cooked egg. That air space (sometimes known as "the chick's first breath") forms when the inner membrane contracts as the egg cools after it's laid. If you give those membranes a tug, you'll find they're surprisingly strong. They are made partly of keratin, the same protein found in human hair.

Egg white is comprised of water and approximately 40 different proteins that form four alternating bands of thick and thin albumen. Crack open an egg onto a plate and look at it closely. You can probably see at least two bands—thick albumen surrounding the yolk and thin albumen spreading out further on the plate.

The proteins *lysozyme* and *ovotransferrin* inhibit bacterial growth in raw eggs, making the whites less prone to contamination than the yolks. In nature, this protects the chick embryo. Once the shell

Cook's Query

Are brown eggs more nutritious than white eggs?

The color of an eggshell is determined by the breed of hen and doesn't in any way affect the quality or nutritional value of an egg.

is broken, however, the egg is highly susceptible to bacterial growth and these defenses are inadequate to cope with the task. Once out of the shell, raw eggs should be used within two days.

The yolk contains less water and more protein than the white, some fat, and most of the vitamins and minerals of the egg. Its color ranges from just a hint of yellow to a magnificent deep orange, according to the feed and breed of the hen.

At the top of the yolk is a slight depression that's barely noticeable. This is the germ spot, the point at which the sperm enters the egg to fertilize it. The portion of the yolk containing this spot is less dense, so when the egg turns and the chalazae allow the yolk to revolve, the germ spot stays on top, keeping it close to the source of warmth, traditionally the roosting hen.

How Eggs Age

Have you ever dropped an egg into boiling water for poaching, only to have the white wander in every possible direction? As it cooks in stringy, unappetizing threads, you wonder how you're ever going to collect it, let alone serve it. Odds are that troublesome egg had been sitting in your refrigerator or the grocer's for some time.

Try poaching the freshest egg you can find, and the result will be quite different. A very fresh egg white clings tightly to the yolk—an advantage for the cook and definitely more appealing to eat.

How Fresh Is It?

est an egg for freshness by submerging it in a bowl of water. Eggs that are very fresh have a small air cell, so they sink to the bottom and lie on their sides. Older eggs are buoyed by an air pocket that gets bigger as water evaporates through the pores in the shell. These eggs tilt large end up in the water. Eggs keep four to five weeks beyond their packing date without significant loss in quality. After that time, if they've been constantly refrigerated, they are more likely to become dry due to moisture loss than they are to spoil.

Like all of us, eggs change as they age. From a cook's perspective, these changes bring about small but noteworthy differences in an egg's cooking properties.

As an egg ages, the yolk flattens and breaks more easily and the white becomes thinner. Knowing this, whenever we're on one of the West Coast islands not far from Vancouver, we buy eggs from a favorite farm. These eggs are so fresh they make prize-winning poached eggs! Each deep yellow yolk stands high, and the white is thick and contained, so the egg poaches to a neat package. And adding a little salt or an acid such as vinegar to the cooking water encourages the eggs to coagulate at a lower temperature, which helps keep them very tender. (Prolonged cooking takes protein from firm to rubbery as protein molecules bond together and squeeze out moisture.)

Older eggs may not be good for poaching, but they make great hard-cooked eggs. At one time or another, you've probably had difficulty peeling the shell from a hard-cooked egg. That's because the shells cling tightly to the membranes inside a very fresh egg. As an egg ages, air passes through its porous shell, enlarging the space between the membranes. That space is a great ally when it comes to peeling. So a chilled hard-cooked egg that was more than a week old before cooking is much easier to peel than one that was recently laid. Peel a fresh hard-cooked egg while it's still warm rather than letting it cool.

Eggs are highly perishable, and should always be kept refrigerated. According to The American Egg Board, an egg that's spent a week in the refrigerator is fresher than an egg left at room temperature for a day. Since an eggshell has between 7,000 and 17,000 pores, eggs easily absorb odors from other foods. Storing them in their cartons is the best way to reduce the chance of having your eggs taste like last night's pizza. Notice they are usually packed with the tapered end down, which keeps the yolk well positioned in the center of the white, in case you want to hard-cook perfect eggs.

Realizing the mistake, she flung open the microwave's door just as the egg exploded. Imagine the mess. Even the kitchen ceiling had to be repainted.

It is easiest to separate yolks from whites when the egg is cold. However, it's often not optimal to cook with cold eggs. Added to creamed fat and sugar, a cold egg causes a cake batter to separate, giving it a curdled appearance. Egg whites are also easiest to beat to a foam when they're at room temperature, rather than cold.

The process of warming eggs presents a dilemma for the cook. Remove them from the refrigerator—but for two hours at the most. They're prone to spoilage if left out longer. Some cooks suggest that removing eggs from the refrigerator 30 minutes ahead of time warms them sufficiently.

When we forget to do that, we often use an unconventional method of warming eggs—seven seconds per large egg in the microwave—just enough to take the cold away. Anne once paid dearly for taking this potentially dangerous shortcut, however, when she inadvertently pressed one minute and seven seconds instead. Realizing the mistake, she flung open the microwave's door just as the egg exploded. Imagine the mess. Even the kitchen ceiling had to be repainted. A much safer way is to cover the eggs with warm water for 10 to 15 minutes. Or separate yolks from whites while they're cold, then place them in bowls over warm water.

Storing Yolks and Whites

Once the contents of an egg are separated from the protective mechanism of the shell, they are a perfect moist, low-acid medium for bacterial growth and should be used quickly.

Egg whites can be kept covered in the refrigerator for two days. It's a real bonus, however, that leftover egg whites freeze well, so you can accumulate enough for a favorite cake or meringue; one large egg white is approximately 2 tablespoons (25 ml). Use a heavy freezer bag or freeze the whites in ice cube trays and transfer them to a freezer bag when they're solid, so you can defrost only the number you need. Thaw frozen whites in the refrigerator and use them immediately.

To keep whole egg yolks, cover them with a small amount of cold water, then a lid to keep them from drying, and refrigerate. Pour off the water and use them within two days. For longer storage, think about how you plan to use them. If they're destined for something sweet, add 1½ teaspoons (7 ml) sugar or corn syrup to every four yolks. If they'll be added to something savory like scrambled eggs or omelets, add ⅛ teaspoon (½ ml) salt for every four yolks. Then freeze them. The addition of salt or sugar helps keep the yolk from becoming grainy as it freezes.

Whole raw eggs cracked from their shell can also be frozen for use in baking. Beat just enough to blend the yolk and white, pour into an airtight container, and freeze.

Try a Little Tenderness

A "boiled egg" may be part of the breakfast tradition in many households, but boiling is a miserable way to treat an egg. Because high heat toughens protein, the major constituent of eggs, boiling quickly changes an egg from a tender gel to a resilient sphere.

You might be surprised to learn that egg white solidifies between 140°F (60°C) and 149°F (65°C)—far below water's boiling

Oops! Which Eggs Are Hard-Cooked?

Spinning reveals the difference. Take a raw egg and a hard-cooked egg, spin each egg rapidly for a while, then stop it abruptly. When you let go, the raw egg will slowly start to move by itself. The hard-cooked egg will stay put. Because the components in a raw egg are different densities, the egg tends to wobble reluctantly rather than spin quickly like the hard-cooked egg. And when the egg is stopped, the fluid inside continues to rotate. The hard-cooked egg with its solid components is able to come to an abrupt stop.

point. Egg yolk coagulates between 149°F (65°C) and 158°F (70°C), a temperature higher than egg whites because the yolk's protein structure is different and not as sensitive to heat. When an egg is in boiling water, the intense heat promotes extensive protein bonding, so it solidifies quickly and changes to a texture that's best described as "rubbery." Cooked gently, eggs are firm but still tender. They not only taste better, they're easier to digest.

When eggs are overcooked, you'll often see a greenish film on the outside of the yolk. With excessive heat, sulfur and hydrogen from the egg white bond to form hydrogen sulfide gas (that rotten egg smell). This gas gravitates to the coldest part of the egg, which of course is the center. The iron in the yolk quickly bonds with the sulfur to form a coating of iron sulfide on the yolk. It's harmless, but unappetizing. You can avoid it by hard-cooking eggs just to the point where they coagulate completely—and no more. Plunging them immediately into cold water also helps, because it stops the cooking process and the cold pulls the hydrogen sulfide gas away from the yolk and toward the rapidly cooling shell.

To "soft-cook" an egg in its shell, cover it with warm water, bring it to a boil, then turn off the heat. Let stand four to five minutes. Add an extra two minutes cooking time to eggs taken directly from the refrigerator. For hard-cooked eggs, bring the water and eggs to a boil, and turn the heat off for 25 minutes. Or, if you're in a hurry as we usually are, simmer (but just barely) soft-cooked eggs for three minutes and hard-cooked eggs for 15 to 20 minutes. Immerse hard-cooked eggs in cold running water.

Although eggs are always less prone to cracking if you bring them to room temperature before cooking, it does seem that some eggs are more resistant to cracking than others. Some eggshells have larger pores that allow air to escape more easily. Watch an egg carefully as it warms in the cooking water and you may see a little stream of air bubbles escaping from the large end. This is air that has expanded as the egg heats and has found its way out through the tiny pores in the shell. If pressure builds faster than the air can escape, the shell cracks.

Try making a pinhole in the air space at the large end of the egg. This facilitates a quick exit of air, reducing the pressure that builds inside the eggshell. The pinhole also has another advantage. When the air leaves while the egg is still liquid, the egg white fills the air pocket, and you'll end up with a perfectly oval hard-cooked egg, rather than one with a dent in the fat end.

When you heat an egg, the air inside expands. If you make a hole in the large end of the shell, you provide the expanding air with an escape route, and the egg is less likely to crack. As you heat the egg, you'll see a stream of bubbles escaping through the hole.

See for Yourself

Effects of gentle versus high heat on egg proteins

Prepare a baked custard mixture, pour it into individual serving dishes, and place all except one in a shallow pan with hot water halfway up the sides of the custard cups. Place the remaining custard on the oven rack beside the water bath, and bake all the custards the same length of time. If you peek in the oven when the custards are almost cooked, that poor lone custard will probably be boiling! Compare this custard to one cooked in the water bath. When they're cooled, turn each onto a plate and examine it carefully. Chances are the custard without the benefit of the water bath is full of little holes and oozing liquid. Taste it and you'll find the texture is quite rubbery. That's because the egg proteins have coagulated, then toughened, squeezing out liquid as they're exposed to prolonged heat.

The same phenomenon occurs when an egg is cooked in a sizzling frying pan. The white gets tough and rubbery and has little holes throughout where water has leaked from the coagulating white. Even for frying eggs, gentle heat is preferable.

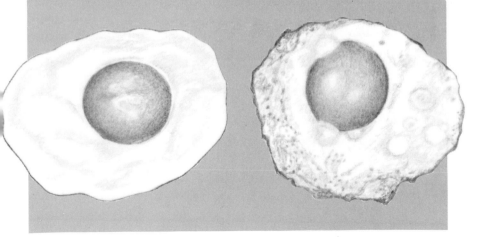

Ties That Bind

Blending eggs with milk and allowing them to coagulate without being stirred forms an interlocking network that traps liquid in a delicate gel. (One whole egg or two egg yolks will gel 1 cup (250 ml) of milk.) This is the essence of a custard—baked to a tender gel for dishes like crème caramel, crème brûlée, and quiche. If custard is stirred gently while cooking, it becomes a thickened custard sauce, or crème anglaise. The calcium and chloride ions in milk also contribute to the gel, and milk whey proteins play a minor role in helping the custard set.

Cooking at too high a temperature or for too long toughens proteins and squeezes out liquid. This makes a baked custard "weep," and a stirred custard curdle.

In both stirred and baked custards, setting happens at temperatures well below boiling. Cooking at too high a temperature or for too long toughens proteins and squeezes out liquid. This makes a baked custard "weep," and a stirred custard curdle—both signs of overcooking.

Baked custards are usually cooked in a hot water bath to slow the cooking process and insulate the egg mixture from direct heat. It also keeps the temperature uniform so the outside doesn't overcook while the inside is still runny.

Stirred custards also benefit from slow heating and gentle stirring, precautions that decrease the chance of curdling. When egg proteins are heated quickly, there's a very small temperature difference (just a few degrees) between thickening and overcooking, so that custards seem to curdle almost instantly. When heated slowly, this range widens to 10°F or more. When the custard coats the back of a metal spoon, it's cooked. Cool immediately so the residual heat in the pan doesn't coagulate the custard further.

Just as egg proteins hold liquid in a gel for custards, eggs can also help bind ingredients together in a variety of meat and vegetable dishes. If you dip a veal cutlet in beaten egg and then in a crumb coating, the coating will cling tightly to the meat. Then the coating insulates the cutlet from the direct heat of the pan and traps evaporating moisture so the meat has a chance to tenderize in moist heat as it cooks.

Stir a raw egg into a casserole and when cooked, it will serve in tidier portions. Similarly, meat loaves are less likely to crumble if an egg is included, as the egg proteins coagulate and hold the mixture together.

Egg proteins work along with starch to form the structure of most cakes and cookies as they coagulate in the oven during baking. The fat in the yolk also keeps baked goods moist. That's why an angel food cake with only egg whites is drier than a chiffon cake, which contains both yolks and beaten whites.

You can also work with egg's structure-forming qualities when substituting beaten egg whites for whole eggs in fat-reduced cakes. If you're not happy with the result, consider adding a quarter of the whites unbeaten. While the beaten whites raise the structure, the unbeaten whites help bind the ingredients together and set the structure of the cake.

It's Upside Down for Cooling Angel Food Cakes

Angel food cakes are so featherlight and airy they seem well-suited to the appetites of more ethereal beings—though those of us more firmly grounded occasionally have the pleasure of enjoying them, too. Recipes for true angel food cakes contain no chemical leavening and very little flour. Beaten egg whites not only form the basis of their delicate structure, they also reach incredible heights in the oven as air bubbles rise and evaporating liquid generates steam during baking. A traditional angel food cake pan always has a center tube to support this delicate batter as it climbs. Once baked, such a fragile framework tends to compress. By turning the pan upside down when the cake is baked, the air cells stay stretched until the structure solidifies as it cools.

Eggs as Leavening

Yorkshire pudding, that old English favorite, and perennially popular popovers both have the reputation of being tricky to make. Indeed, it's hard to imagine how any batter with so much liquid could possibly rise, let alone pop. But popovers and Yorkshire pudding are perceived as difficult only because the role of steam in lifting batters is seldom explained. And the role of eggs in forming the structure is underrated.

Traditional recipes for Yorkshire pudding include just flour, milk, eggs, and a little salt blended together to a smooth batter the thickness of whipping cream. Egg proteins and starch from the small amount of flour in the batter form a cohesive but delicate, easily lifted framework. The power for lifting this framework comes from steam generated by the evaporating liquid. When liquid turns to watervapor, it expands to more than 1,400 times its original volume. The top pops with ease, as steam lifts the partly baked batter. A metal pan conducts heat better than glass. To jump-start steam formation, and to ensure the sides cook quickly, be sure to preheat the pan in a hot oven before adding the batter.

A popover's dramatic rise demonstrates the power of steam generated by evaporating liquid.

The Beaten Egg

It's fun to watch the faces of children as they observe the transformation of viscous egg whites to billowy mountains of foam for the first time. The whites increase up to eight times their original volume.

When an egg is fresh, its proteins are tightly coiled. As we beat egg whites for a meringue or soufflé, air pulled into the fluid whites disperses as minute bubbles in the water portion of the white. As this liquid stretches around the bubbles, it's aided by proteins, which uncoil much like stretched rubber bands. As they do this, they bond loosely with other unraveling proteins, creating a mesh that holds a liquid film around the bubble. When a foam retains air without collapsing it's called stable. However, as you've no doubt experienced, even a stable egg white foam doesn't last long.

Recipes often specify a special consistency of beaten egg whites. Here are the three characteristic stages—and one beyond.

1. **Foamy Stage**—The egg white is lightly whipped. It's still frothy and fluid and does not hold a peak. Bubbles are large and still break easily.

2. **Soft Peak Stage**—The foam is white, moist, shiny and still flows in the bowl. As beating divides large air cells, the bubbles become smaller and the mixture thickens. When the beater is lifted, peaks form but fold over at the top. It's at this stage that you can start adding sugar gradually for meringues. The foam reaches maximum stability—yet it still has enough stretch that the whites can inflate as hot air rises in the oven. The soft peak stage is ideal for most cooking purposes. If no sugar is added, you usually stop beating egg whites at this point.

3. **Stiff Peak Stage**—The foam no longer flows in the bowl. Peaks form and remain upright when the beaters are lifted. A spatula cut through the foam leaves a deep cleft with straight sides. At this stage, the foam is at the maximum volume that's useful for cooking. Unless sugar has been added to stabilize it, there is very little room for expansion in the oven.

4. Dry Foam Stage—Though the foam still expands, you've gone too far. The foam is dry, curdled-looking, and has lost its shine. When beaters are lifted, the foam breaks rather than peaks, and moisture oozes out. Just like rubber bands, egg whites won't stretch indefinitely, so an overbeaten egg foam collapses easily, becoming lumpy and resistant to blending with other ingredients.

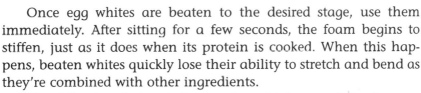

Once egg whites are beaten to the desired stage, use them immediately. After sitting for a few seconds, the foam begins to stiffen, just as it does when its protein is cooked. When this happens, beaten whites quickly lose their ability to stretch and bend as they're combined with other ingredients.

The following factors influence how high egg whites become and how long they can stand without breaking.

Older egg whites have a lower surface tension, which means that the forces that hold the molecules in the liquid portion of the whites are not as strong as they are in fresh egg whites. Therefore, eggs that are older can be beaten to a foam more readily than eggs that are thicker and very fresh. Whites at room temperature also can be

Compare the meringue produced by egg whites contaminated by a touch of egg yolk (right) and the meringue produced by yolk-free egg whites. The fat in egg yolk prevents the formation of the protein bonds that make a meringue fluffy.

Cook's Query
How do you "fold in" egg whites?

This technique for adding beaten egg whites to a heavier mixture, such as a batter or thickened sauce, is always done by hand so as not to break the air bubbles. It's designed so beaten whites don't collapse through ordinary stirring when you are making cakes, puddings, and soufflés. Using the edge of a large rubber spatula, cut down through the center of the mixture to the bottom of the bowl. Draw the spatula up the side of the bowl, then turn it over, and cut down through the center again. Turn the bowl a quarter turn each time and continue folding (never stirring) until there are no streaks of white remaining in the mixture.

If you find that little lumps of egg white seem to linger and are difficult to incorporate, you've likely beaten the whites too zealously. If they're too stiff, the coagulated protein squeezes out moisture, leaving them dry and unable to expand. It's actually preferable to underbeat egg whites than to overbeat them.

Cook's Query
Can overbeaten egg whites be salvaged?

All is not lost. As long as you haven't added any other ingredients, you can usually resurrect a foam by adding an extra egg white and beating just until the mixture looks glossy and forms peaks again.

beaten to a foam more easily. Egg whites that have been frozen, as well as dehydrated whites, form good foams with excellent volume. Research suggests that fresh eggs form a more stable foam that holds longer before it collapses. For meringues and soufflés, we prefer older eggs with their greater volume.

Even one drop of egg yolk in the white decreases the potential volume by one-third, as even this tiny amount of fat inhibits the formation of a good foam. This means that not only must you take great care when separating the white from the yolk, but also that you beat eggs in metal or glass bowls. Plastic bowls tend to retain traces of fat that are very difficult to remove.

Check your beaters, too! Beaters and whisks with thin wires form smaller air cells in egg whites than beaters with blades. A myriad of tiny cells will help your meringue or soufflé rise higher and have a better texture than fewer but larger air cells.

Sugar is one of your best allies in creating a stable egg white foam. It reduces the chances of overbeating, partly because its presence interferes with protein molecules finding one another and bonding. When bonding happens slowly, egg whites are more difficult to overbeat.

Sugar also reinforces a foam because it dissolves during beating and bonds with water, holding moisture in the film surrounding the air bubbles. This keeps proteins moist and allows them to bend. If proteins dry out too quickly during baking, they become rigid and unable to stretch as the air bubbles expand.

Can Curdled Hollandaise Sauce Be Saved?

A broken emulsion isn't a complete disaster. Providing you haven't overcooked the egg yolks, it can be formed again. Simply whisk the broken hollandaise gradually into another beaten egg yolk. Then serve it immediately. It won't be quite as delicate, but most guests are so impressed with home-made hollandaise, they probably won't notice.

Don't try to store this sauce, as it's the ideal medium for bacterial growth. And because oil and water expand at different rates, extremes in temperature also cause hollandaise to separate. Refrigeration doesn't work. The butter solidifies and separates. And reheating causes curdling. Once you've made hollandaise sauce, serve it as quickly as possible. Or keep it warm in a scrupulously clean wide-neck thermos while you do the last-minute meal preparations.

Before adding sugar, be sure to beat the egg whites to the beginning of the soft peak stage. If added too soon, sugar removes water from the proteins, so incorporating air into the foam becomes more difficult and the volume of the foam is smaller. Or you may not get any foam at all.

Acids, such as cream of tartar, also contribute to the stability of egg foams by lowering the pH so protein molecules attract, rather than repel each other. Add $\frac{1}{16}$ teaspoon cream of tartar (.25 ml) per white after the whites are beaten to the foamy stage. Though lemon juice and vinegar are often-used acidic ingredients, they also add extra liquid, and the protein network that forms during beating is weaker.

Bringing Fat and Liquid Together

Just as the keystone at the apex of an arch locks the whole together, eggs are pivotal ingredients, creating liaisons between fat and liquid. Mayonnaise and most cake batters are emulsions. This means they contain both fat and water-based liquids—components that normally won't stay mixed. Yet when egg yolks are included, these two ingredients blend together in a creamy mixture that looks quite unlike either fat or liquid.

The egg yolk's ability to hold unlikely neighbors together is due to the presence of emulsifiers like lecithin, which comprises about 30 percent of the yolk. Emulsifiers act as the bridge that joins the water portion with the fat in a cake batter, so it stays cohesive and holds air well. Lecithin also surrounds the droplets of oil suspended in the liquids included in mayonnaise, so once it's thickened, it stays that way. Egg yolks serve the same purpose in hollandaise and bernaise sauces, although the proportions of ingredients in these emulsions make them much less stable.

There's no question that the humble little egg is handy in the kitchen. No wonder it has developed the reputation as the jack-of-all-trades in cooking.

Cook's Query

How do egg whites work to clarify a broth?

Egg whites whisked into a broth act much like a magnet, attracting particles that would potentially cloud the broth, and trapping them as the egg protein coagulates in the heat. Then the whites rise to the top forming a crust-like layer of foam which can be scooped easily from the surface, leaving a clear broth below.

The Alchemy of Granules & Powders

ooking doesn't change base metals into gold. But it does transform very common ingredients into some of the finest meals you have ever eaten. In that sense, it is a sort of alchemy—a very successful one—resting on the underpinnings of science and understanding.

Granules and powders—including baking soda, baking powder, sugar, and salt—are involved in some of the most fascinating processes in cooking. Because cooks don't call these common ingredients by their scientific names, they are seldom thought of as chemical compounds. But understanding the interactions of these common ingredients can help make you a better baker, fix a recipe that flops, or make a good recipe even better.

You'll notice only subtle differences among the granules and powders in your kitchen. Some reflect light. Some are transparent. Some feel rougher than others. A few taste perfectly dreadful. But if you take them out of their containers, baking powder, baking soda, sugar, and salt look surprisingly similar.

We're always struck by what innocuous little piles these chemicals seem to be—until they're moistened. Then suddenly each has specific functions that set it well apart from the others.

Along with baking powder and baking soda, in this chapter we'll also talk about the oldest leaven of them all, yeast. Modern cooks often use a granular form of this ancient leaven—so we've taken the liberty of including it here—though its appearance as a granule is really a disguise.

Some Powders Make Light of Baking

These powders tell it like it is—they really are "baking powders." But amidst their bubbles and fizz, baking powder and baking soda also cause some confusion. If you've ever wondered how these powders work, how they differ, and why some recipes call for both, you're not alone.

Amidst their bubbles and fizz, baking powder and baking soda also cause some confusion.

In batters and doughs, baking soda and baking powder react chemically to make millions of tiny bubbles of carbon dioxide. Because these powders work quickly, they're used to leaven baked goods with a delicate structure, ones that rise easily as the gas is produced. That's why muffins and loaves leavened this way are often referred to as *quick breads*.

The chemical name for baking soda is sodium bicarbonate and its chemical formula is $NaHCO_3$. Baking soda is an alkali, or a base, and it reacts with acid to make carbon dioxide. So the most important thing to remember about baking soda is that it works best in partnership with an acidic ingredient. Without acid, baking soda can't properly do its job.

Cook's Queries

Why do some recipes call for both baking powder and baking soda?

Often the quantity of baking soda needed to balance the acid ingredient isn't sufficient to leaven the entire amount of flour in a recipe. Baking powder adds extra leavening so the dough rises sufficiently.

Can I add extra baking powder if I want extra-high muffins?

No, because it won't work! Too much leaven overinflates batters, weakens the structure, and causes collapse...and an even heavier texture. A general rule of thumb is that 1 to 2 teaspoons (5 to 10 ml) of baking powder, or ¼ teaspoon (1 ml) of baking soda plus ½ cup (125 ml) of an acidic ingredient (such as sour milk, yogurt, applesauce, etc.), leavens 1 cup (250 ml) of flour. The amount varies according to the ingredients and how they're mixed. For example, batters that contain lots of air, because egg whites have been beaten separately, need less leavening than dense batters that are laden with dried fruits and heavy grains.

There's logic in those treasured old recipes for scones or chocolate cake that call for sour milk or sour cream, as these ingredients are acids. Coupled with their unique flavors, they are perfect partners for baking soda.

Look through a batch of cookie or muffin recipes that call for baking soda and see if you can identify the acid. You might be in for some surprises.

Knowing that you need acid to react with baking soda will help you understand why some recipes fail. In most recipes, the acid and the baking soda balance so neither is left behind in excess. Often,

Active Ingredients

The following are commonly used with baking soda in leavening.

The number at the left tells you the pH, a measurement of acidity. The lower the number, the more acidic the food. (To learn more about the concept of pH, see page 28.)

2.0–2.4	Limes, lemons, lemon juice
2.4–3.4	Vinegar
2.7	Cranberries
2.9–3.2	Rhubarb
2.9–3.3	Apples
2.9–3.6	Raspberries
3.2–3.7	Blueberries
3.3	Apricots, blackberries
3.4–4.0	Orange juice
3.5–5.5	Honey
4.3–4.4	Yogurt, sour cream
4.5–5.1	Buttermilk
4.6	Bananas
5.0	Carrots, pumpkin
5.0–5.4	Molasses
5.3–6.0	Natural cocoa and chocolate
6.4–7.8	Dutch-processed cocoa (treated to reduce its acidity)
6.5–7.0	Overripe bananas

however, we come across recipes using baking soda that contain no acidic counterpart. Carbon dioxide is still produced, but not with the same vigor. The alkaline baking soda that is left unneutralized has a soapy, bitter taste. The alkalinity also causes color changes, yellowing the pigments in flour, accelerating browning, and altering the familiar colors of chocolate and molasses.

Cream of tartar, an acid in the form of a granule, is sometimes used to complete the reaction with baking soda. This fascinating crystal, a by-product of the wine industry, was a component in the first commercial baking powders.

We chuckled when we read that those first baking powders were advertised as a means of reducing nervous tension in the kitchen.

We chuckled when we read that those first baking powders were advertised as a means of reducing nervous tension in the kitchen. But we agree that never knowing for sure whether your baking will rise could indeed be stressful.

You can duplicate this early type of baking powder by combining one part baking soda with two parts cream of tartar. When you make a batter using this homemade baking powder, mixing should be brief, so carbon dioxide is captured within the batter or dough as it sets in the oven. If your mixing is leisurely, leavening gases will be released too soon and you'll be left with muffins that are very compact. Homemade hockey pucks anyone?

Today, commercial baking powder is still composed of baking soda plus one or more acids. However, baking powders are now carefully designed to react more slowly than the original tartrate baking powders, allowing more time to get those muffins into the oven before leavening begins.

Read the label on a can of baking powder and you'll find it contains baking soda, cornstarch, and one or more dry acids. Cornstarch absorbs moisture and keeps the baking soda and acid from reacting during storage. It also acts as a filler that standardizes brands of baking powder so they all release approximately the same amount of carbon dioxide.

Heavy Banana Bread?

Cooks often relegate bananas that are too ripe for eating to banana bread. And why not? They're sweet and full of flavor, just a little too mushy for even devoted banana eaters. The trouble is that as bananas ripen, their acidity decreases (see the pH chart on page 57), so their reaction in partnership with baking soda is a weak one. A good banana bread recipe ensures adequate leavening by using both baking powder and baking soda.

Double-acting baking powder often contains two acid components that react independently. A phosphate component reacts during mixing with sodium bicarbonate and a liquid. The second component, often a sulfate, reacts when the batter or dough is heated, creating another surge of leavening in the oven.

Or a double-acting baking powder may contain one acid component that reacts quickly to create carbon dioxide plus a new acid salt. When heated, this salt combines with the remaining sodium bicarbonate in a chain reaction that completes the leavening. This makes double-acting baking powder particularly useful for doughs that must stand or chill before baking, or large quantities that take extra preparation time before they reach the oven.

Because brands of baking powder vary in the rate at which they work and the ultimate pH they create in the batter or dough, you may notice subtle changes in the texture and flavor of your baking when you try different brands.

The carbon dioxide produced by leavens works in conjunction with both air and steam. Any process that adds air—creaming shortening, beating eggs, kneading dough, sifting flour—helps create a honeycomb of air pockets, which bubbles of carbon dioxide gas inflate. With your help, air, steam, and carbon dioxide accomplish with ease the daunting task of pushing doughs to remarkable heights.

Yeast, the Friendly Fungus

Baking soda and baking powder react chemically to produce the carbon dioxide that makes baked goods rise. In contrast, yeast is living and feeds on dough, producing carbon dioxide as a by-product.

Sue often says that you can only really know yeast by making bread by hand (albeit with a little mechanical help in the initial mixing stage). You can help the yeast thrive by providing the right conditions. And it will respond. Think about the warmth that yeast generates in dough as it does its job and the swoosh of gases that are released when dough is punched down. Because yeast is a living ingredient, making bread is always different, and therefore never loses its fascination.

Yeast is a member of the fungus family—a strange and ancient kind of life. Fungi range from microscopic single cells, like yeast, to large mushrooms and toadstools, as well as molds.

No one has ever tallied all the different strains of yeast. Many are wild and constantly surround us in the air and soil. Over time, strains of yeast change and mutate—they also vary throughout the world. Yeast not only makes your bread rise, these useful fungi are also responsible for the fermentation of wine and beer.

Two forms of yeast are used in baking: moist pressed cakes that you may remember your grandmother using (a form that many bakers still use) and dehydrated granules. Both are strains of the

Here's what you're working with when making bread. These single-celled fungi are so tiny that just 1 gram (⅛₈ oz) holds 25 billion cells. It's mind-boggling to consider that each time you make bread you use five times more yeast cells than the population of the earth.

Cook's Query

How do older types of dry yeast differ from newer ones?

T he newer quick-rising types of yeast don't need activating first. Because of their small particle size, they dissolve easily within the dough, without being reconstituted separately. Fast-rising forms of yeast call for warmer water because the dry ingredients insulate the yeast so the entire mass of dough must become sufficiently warm to activate the yeast cells. The newer types of yeast are also more active so they rise more quickly.

microorganism *Saccharomyces cerevisiae,* well-suited to baking because it breaks down starches and ferments sugars, creating carbon dioxide and alcohol as waste products.

Think of pellets of yeast, in their air-tight package, as lying in suspended animation. Like all living things, they need moisture, food, and warmth in order to grow.

The first step is activating yeast cells by soaking them in liquid. But different forms of yeast have varying temperature preferences.

You've probably noticed that when yeast granules are in warm water, they always dissolve but sometimes don't bubble. Just like other living things, before it becomes very active, yeast needs food. Try adding a teaspoon of sugar and watch the bubbles appear. (If the water temperature is right and nothing happens after 10 minutes, the yeast is too old or it's dead. Throw it away and start again.)

Yeast's first food preference is sugar and then starches. If the right food isn't handy, yeast manipulates its alternatives in ingenious ways. For instance, it prefers simple sugars, such as glucose and fructose. If only granulated sugar, a more complex form, is present, an enzyme called *invertase,* found in yeast, facilitates the breakdown of table sugar into the simpler forms yeast prefers.

Yeast is Fussy About Temperature

400°F — 205°C	**300–400°F (150–205°C)** Surface temperature of a browning crust.
	200°F (100°C) Interior temperature of a loaf of just-baked bread.
300°F — 150°C	**130–140°F (55–60°C)** Yeast cells die (thermal death point).
	120–130°F (49–55°C) Water temperature for activating yeast designed to be mixed with the dry ingredients in a recipe.
200°F — 100°C	**105–115°F (41–46°C)** Temperature of water for dry yeast reconstituted with water and sugar.
	100°F (38°C) or lower When yeast is mixed with water at too low a temperature, an amino acid called glutathione leaks from the cell walls, making doughs sticky and hard to handle.
140°F — 60°C	**95°F (35°C)** Temperature for liquids used to dissolve compressed yeast.
130°F 120°F — 50°C 110°F 100°F — 40°C	**80–90°F (27–32°C)** Optimum temperature range for yeast to grow and reproduce at dough fermentation stage—a much lower temperature than that required to initially activate it.
90°F — 30°C 80°F	**70–80°F (21–27°C)** Recommended water temperature for bread machines.
70°F — 20°C 60°F 50°F	**40°F (4°C)** Recommended refrigerator temperature. Used directly from the fridge, yeast is too cold to work properly.
40°F — 4°C	

Yeast also contains the enzyme *maltase*, which helps break down some of the starch in flour to a simple sugar that yeast can use. This only happens, however, after the supply of glucose and fructose has been exhausted. Yeast must take this extra step in true French breads, which do not contain sugar. That's one reason such breads rise more slowly.

Each Step in Bread Making Helps Yeast Do Its Job

Once the dough is mixed and kneading begins, the elasticity develops in flour so the dough becomes strong enough to hold the carbon dioxide as it's slowly produced by the yeast. As the volume of gas increases, the dough stretches and lifts. Once the dough is satiny smooth and you can feel it resisting as you knead, it's left to rise at warm temperatures. Yeast grows best at the temperature of a pleasant summer day—about 80°F (27°C). But it also works slowly. Many bakers believe that a long, slow rise at slightly lower temperatures (75°F/24°C) develops a fuller flavor in the finished loaf.

This period, called *fermentation*, allows yeast to get on with its life processes, which, from the perspective of cooks, is considered to be the business of lifting. As yeast ferments, it also makes doughs easier to handle, and the alcohols and organic acids it produces create new aromas and flavors.

Cook's Query

Why do some yeast breads include mashed potatoes?

Mashed potatoes contain cooked granules that are easily converted by enzymes in flour to maltose, a sugar yeast uses as food. Even cooking water that contains starch left behind by the potatoes is often used in yeast doughs.

Initially, dough rises slowly, but it picks up momentum as fermentation proceeds. So a second or final rising period (often referred to as "proofing") always takes less time than the first.

Punching the dough down after its initial rising breaks up large pockets of gas so the dough becomes evenly inflated. It also redistributes the yeast and its food, and equalizes temperature differences throughout the dough.

As yeast breads bake, leavening gases are trapped in the dough. Moisture turns to steam, a powerful natural leaven that also helps add volume. As water evaporates from the dough, the structure of the loaf solidifies. Heat eventually kills the yeast and inactivates its enzymes. Warm yeasty odors wafting from the oven mix with alcohol, a waste product of yeast's metabolism. You can sometimes smell the alcohol as it evaporates during baking. As you lift those crusty, browned loaves from the oven, it's satisfying to see that once again the tiny friendly fungus has done its job well.

The Many Facets of Salt

There are few cooking ingredients with as much drama and violence in their history as salt. When salt was scarce, wars were fought. Rulers jealously guarded salt monopolies. At times, salt was traded equally, ounce for ounce, with gold.

Salt in its mineral form is known as *halite,* formed from the elements sodium and chlorine. In moderation its consumption is essential, for salt lost from the body must be replenished. Sodium plays a role in the contraction of muscles, including the heart, and helps send electrical impulses along the nerves. Salt is also one of the gate-keepers regulating the amount of water that constantly moves between body cells and their surrounding fluid.

As one of the world's oldest and now most plentiful seasonings, salt brings its unique properties to our tables from a variety of fascinating sources. Sea salt is harvested from the ocean; rock salt is mined from the earth where ancient seas have dried. Most North American table salt is evaporated from heavily concentrated brines formed when water is pumped into salt formations.

An Index to Salts

- **TABLE SALT** is almost pure sodium chloride, refined to remove traces of other minerals. It's mixed with an anticaking agent to keep it from clumping, so it flows freely.

  Some countries have legislated that potassium iodide be added to table salt. Supplementing salt with iodine has virtually eliminated goiter, a swelling of the thyroid gland. Table salt also contains a small amount of sugar. Without it, the iodine would oxidize and turn the salt yellow.

- **KOSHER SALT** is coarse, irregularly shaped crystals produced from evaporated brine under strict conditions set by the Orthodox Jewish faith. It contains no additives or iodine. If you want to use a comparable salt and are not attempting to satisfy Jewish dietary laws, coarse salt for pickling can be substituted.

- **COARSE SALT FOR PICKLING** contains no additives since they cause cloudiness in pickling brines. Some cooks consider coarse and Kosher salt to taste less salty than table salt. But if the salts are equally pure, there is no difference in saltiness. What makes the difference is particle size. Smaller salt crystals have a larger surface area and a saltier taste.

- **SEA SALT** can be purchased in various degrees of fineness. Some feel it has a fresher, lighter taste than table salt. But purity can vary according to the source. Fine sea salt can be used interchangeably with table salt, though sea salt does not contain enough iodine to meet the body's need for iodine.

- **ROCK SALT** may contain impurities and levels of anticaking agents that exceed the standards allowed for food consumption. But untreated rock salt is commonly associated with churning old-fashioned ice cream and sometimes forms a dramatic background of crystals for displaying oysters on the half shell.

Hold the Salt

There are times when it's best to delay the addition of salt. Don't add salt to egg whites as you beat them, since salt draws water from the whites, promoting coagulation, increasing whipping time, and decreasing the volume and stability of the foam. Omit the salt in marinades, since it draws moisture from the surface of meat, leaving it less moist. And though there's lots of debate about this one, we prefer to add salt to broiled and roasted meat after it has browned. Avoid adding salt to a sauce or stock that will be reduced, adding it only if necessary once the right consistency has been reached.

"Just a pinch" is a familiar phrase that no doubt arose because salt plays a curious role in heightening the natural flavors of food even when it doesn't add any dimension of saltiness. The flavors of sweet foods like cakes, cookies, and icing can benefit from a few grains of salt.

This mechanical salt harvester is scraping salt from a crystallizer bed at a Cargill Salt processing plant. The harvester pours the salt into railroad cars. Cargill Salt harvests one million tons of salt each year at its two plants on San Francisco Bay.

One of salt's oldest functions in cooking is to preserve food. We still use salt in curing meats, making butter, and pickling. Salty surroundings (particularly salty, acidic surroundings) discourage the growth of microorganisms responsible for food spoilage and food poisoning. In a salty environment, microorganisms lose water through osmosis (see page 16) and are unable to grow and reproduce.

Cook's Query

Why is salt added to the ice when making ice cream the old-fashioned way?

When our children were little, we had an old-fashioned ice cream churn, which we shared back and forth between our two families. As one of the children layered the coarse salt and crushed ice into the wooden bucket, this question often arose. The ice melts as it absorbs heat from the ice cream mixture in the metal canister. Gradually, the coarse salt dissolves in that ice water to form a brine. Salt plus ice water is colder than ice water alone.

To understand why salty ice water is colder than plain ice water, you need to look at what's happening on the molecular level. In ice water, water molecules break free of the ice crystals and become liquid water. These molecules absorb energy from their surroundings. Other water molecules are rejoining the ice crystals, a process that releases energy. In ice water, the energy absorbed by molecules that are breaking free is balanced by the energy released by molecules that are rejoining the ice at 32°F (0°C), the freezing point of water.

The presence of salt cuts down on the number of water molecules that rejoin the ice crystals. Water molecules keep leaving the ice, but fewer rejoin. That upsets the energy balance, and the temperature drops below the normal freezing point of water.

The very cold brine absorbs energy from the ice cream mixture, and eventually, the ice cream mixture reaches its freezing point. As the beater turns, the ice cream mixture churns into a collection of tiny frozen crystals.

Cook's Query

Is it important to add salt to the water for boiling vegetables and pasta?

Salt raises the boiling point of water by one or two degrees. So vegetables and pasta cooked in boiling water without salt may take an extra few minutes, since they're cooking in water that's at a lower temperature. Salted water makes both pasta and vegetables slightly firmer and perhaps less moist, but it does add flavor. It's a matter of personal preference. Vegetables such as artichokes, beets, celery, chard, kale, and spinach are naturally high in sodium so these vegetables can easily be cooked without salt.

In cheese making, salt is used to draw liquid whey from slabs of cheese curd. At the back of our favorite Greek food store are piles of large, white pails containing different types of feta cheese, each aging in its own salty brine. Above them is a hand-printed sign listing dodonis, alpha, and at least twelve others, each characterized by its crumbly or smooth texture, degree of saltiness, and whether it's made from cow's, sheep's, or goat's milk. Brine aging is just one of several ways salt is added to cheese. Sometimes it's mixed with the curds before they are pressed into large blocks. Or it may be rubbed on the outside of cheeses after they're formed into blocks or wheels. In cheese making, salt not only suppresses the growth of spoilage bacteria, it also slows the action of starter bacteria so the process of ripening cheese from a rubbery to a crumbly texture takes place gradually.

The role that salt plays in yeast breads is also complex. We still remember the flash of recognition on the face of a lady in one of our classes when we talked about what salt does in bread dough. She had tried to make salt-free bread for her husband, who was on a restricted diet. Her attempts to eliminate salt had resulted in a disastrous mess of sticky dough that seemed to rise with lightning speed. The reasons for this were apparent as we explained that salt slows the rate at which yeast ferments and also retards the action of enzymes which break down gluten and make the dough sticky. Salt-free bread formulas usually reduce the quantity of yeast and water, and often are not of the same high quality as yeast breads that contain some salt.

"Sugar in the Morning, Sugar in the Evening..."

One of the wonderful things about San Francisco on October mornings is the weather—sunny, warm, *no rain*. You can still eat breakfast outside. During a visit there from our home in Vancouver, Canada, while planning this book, we often stopped at a neighborhood coffee bar, not far from the Exploratorium. With mammoth cups of steaming coffee and something freshly baked, we'd sit near big open windows contemplating this project.

As planning becomes writing, and we think back to those mornings, we realize the food we enjoyed was a good example of *disappearance data*, a measure used by the sugar industry to calculate how much sugar goes into our food supply.

For several decades, per-capita sugar consumption has remained close to 90 pounds (41 kg) per year. "Far more than I eat," most of us protest. When you don't bake something yourself, it's easy to forget that the coffee bar's warm muffins, raspberry cream scones, and granola are part of that disappearance data.

Most of the sugar we consume no longer comes from home cooking. It's divided between food industries, home use, restaurants and institutions; nonfood uses of sugar, such as explosives, tobacco,

This photo shows table sugar magnified to 100 times its actual size. When you cream shortening and sugar together, the faces of the sugar crystals drag tiny air bubbles into the shortening.

Other Kinds of Sugar Found in Food

About 6 percent of the sugar we eat is naturally found in foods.

Type of Sugar	Examples	Food Sources
• **Monosaccharides** (Single sugar molecules)	Glucose	Most foods
	Fructose	Fruit, honey
	Galactose	Milk
• **Disaccharides** (Each molecule is made of two single sugar molecules)	Sucrose (glucose + fructose)	Fruits, vegetables, table sugar
	Lactose (glucose + galactose)	Milk
	Maltose (glucose + glucose)	Beer

There are no fruits and vegetables that are truly sugar-free. All contain at least some sucrose, along with fructose and glucose. Many foods, such as legumes, potatoes, rice, bananas, and grains, contain sugars in combination with starches and/or fiber and sugar alcohols.

and pharmaceuticals; and, of course, the loss to waste. Manufactured foods and beverages now account for 70 percent of the sugar consumed, while direct household use has declined. This is a complete reversal of the consumption patterns in the early part of this century.

Sugar, as we know it, is refined from the stalks of sugar cane and the sweet root of the sugar beet. Despite the disparity between these sources, the result is the same when they are processed: sucrose, the chemical name for granulated or table sugar.

Sweetening is sugar's most obvious function. But if you've ever tried cutting the sugar by half in a cake recipe or reducing the amount of sugar in homemade jam, you'll know (by either a very dense cake or a rather runny jam) that sugar is included in cooking for other reasons as well.

Think about your favorite cake recipe. The first instruction probably tells you to cream the shortening and sugar together. As the blades of your mixer whirl, the faces of sugar crystals are dragging very tiny air bubbles into the shortening. Later, leavening gases will enlarge these tiny pockets of air. So a successful beginning plays a part in how evenly textured and how high your cake will be when it comes out of the oven.

Sugar also tenderizes baked goods. You might think of it as an outrageous flirt—happiest when it's attracting water away from its usual companions, the starch and gluten in flour. When water hangs out with sugar instead of gluten, flour's gluten-forming proteins must make do with a limited amount of moisture, and so less gluten develops.

The sugar that you stir into your coffee was probably extracted from sugarcane or sugar beets, the two main sources of refined sugar.

Cook's Query

If sugar affects cooking temperatures, does it also influence freezing?

Mixing water with sugar lowers the temperature at which ice crystals form and restricts their size. Each 1¾ cups sugar per quart of water (approximately 1 liter) lowers the freezing point by 3.3°F (1.86°C). This factor makes ice cream taste cold, feel silky on your tongue, and makes it incredibly refreshing because it freezes at a lower temperature than water. It also makes ice cream more resistant to melting on a blistering hot day. Ices and sherbets don't contain as much butterfat as most ice creams, but they often have more sugar. So they freeze at even lower temperatures than ice cream—and they truly *are* colder. Because freezing temperatures dull the taste buds, frozen desserts often contain more sugar than their sweetness suggests.

(See page 78 for information on gluten.) That's why cakes that are high in sugar have a very tender crumb.

Indirectly, sugar's role as a tenderizer provides another boost to the cake's volume. The more delicate the flour framework, the more easily it lifts when pushed by expanding leavening gases.

But the story doesn't end there. By attracting water away from starch granules, sugar also keeps the batter from setting too quickly. When ingredients in a recipe are well-balanced, setting is delayed until the optimum amount of gas is produced by the leavening agents. Technically, this is called "raising the coagulation point." In more practical terms, the delay in setting allows a cake to rise higher in the oven before the viscous batter changes to a delicate solid.

Sugar also plays a role in browning breads and cakes. There's someone in every family who covets the crust on bread rather than the inside slices. They may not know what causes the browning, crunch, and special flavors, but they do know it's mighty tasty.

A sprinkling of sugar helps create a golden brown top on scones. So does brushing the surface with milk or cream before baking.

Sugar on its own and sugars tied to starches react in the oven with the amino acids in protein ingredients, such as milk and eggs. Cookies tan; cakes deepen in color. You deliberately invite this reaction when you brush the surface of a scone or piecrust with milk or cream. The higher the sugar content, the darker the surface becomes. This is called the *Maillard reaction,* after the French scientist who uncovered the process that causes some foods to change color at high temperatures. The warm colors and rich flavors of roasted coffee beans, barbecued meats, and toasted nuts come from this type of browning.

Browning also takes place when you melt sugar—literally breaking it down to a liquid or molten form by heating it slowly. The process is called *caramelizing.* Sugar becomes a transparent syrup at about 320°F (160°C). Caramelizing begins at about 338°F (170°C) as molten sugar changes in color from transparent, to amber, to a coffee hue. Flavors become rich, deep, and pungent—sometimes with bitter overtones. Many unusual organic compounds are formed as sugar decomposes.

Watch the faces of children as they roast marshmallows over an open fire. Caramelizing can be a dramatic way to cook. In more elegant circumstances, we caramelize sugar to create crème caramel, or the burnt sugar topping on a crème brûlée, adding remarkable new dimensions of color and flavor.

Sugar syrups are also concentrated in candy making. When sugar dissolves in water and the excess water is boiled away, it

Caramelizing Sugar

A t high temperatures, table sugar (or sucrose) breaks down to glucose and fructose. Through caramelization, sugar changes remarkably in character. As you observe the progressive darkening when sugar melts, you are also witnessing the formation of many new and complex compounds responsible for both flavors and aromas.

Caramelizing isn't especially tricky. We think caramelizing dry sugar is the easiest of the caramelizing methods. Other methods involve dissolving the sugar in water and/or adding an acid. Since melted sugar forms an extremely hot and sticky syrup (330–350°F/ 165–175°C) stir with great care, so it doesn't spatter.

Sprinkle ¼ cup (60 ml) granulated sugar evenly on the bottom of a heavy, shallow saucepan. Heat it slowly over low to medium heat and you'll notice it first begins to melt, then gradually becomes a molten syrup. As it gets hotter, it changes to a pale, amber color. Then, within a matter of seconds, it becomes a rich, deep caramel. When it's almost as dark as you'd like, remove the pan from the heat, as it will continue to cook slightly. If you let it get darker, it quickly develops a bitter, then burnt flavor.

If you add ½ cup (125 ml) blanched, slivered almonds to the syrup as it reaches the desired shade of amber, you have made "pralined almonds." Once the almonds are coated with syrup, transfer them to a cookie sheet. Because the almonds tend to clump, pull apart any large clusters once they're cool enough to handle.

One of our favorite winter salads combines pralined almonds with sliced avocado, fresh orange segments, and butter lettuce. Toss just before serving with a light vinaigrette. Any leftover almonds can be pulverized in a blender, stored in an airtight jar, and used in crusts or as toppings for other desserts.

Caramelized sugar is the basis for crème caramel, caramel fillings, sauces, candies, and flavorings. Try adding a little sugar to onions as you finish sautéing them, raise the heat slightly, and you've got a decadent topping for that hamburger.

leaves syrups of specific concentrations. It's handy for cooks that the temperature of the boiling syrup is actually an index of its concentration. And concentration determines how firm the candy will be. The consistency of candy is also influenced by other ingredients, such as corn syrup, acids, cream, or butter, and whether or not the candy is beaten as it cools.

Finally, what about that runny jam? Sugar helps set preserves by interacting with pectin, a carbohydrate that forms an invisible network that sets jams and jellies. But regular pectin couldn't do the job without sugar. Without sufficient sugar, pectin molecules would be more likely to bond with water than with each other. But sugar's affinity for moisture takes some water out of circulation, leaving pectin molecules free to reach each other. As the successful setting of jams and jellies depends on a balance between pectin, acid, and sugar, don't be tempted to reduce sugar in home preserving recipes. Granted you will save calories, but you may also end up with a very runny preserve.

Granules and powders quietly go about their business of creating special effects in cooking.

If you want a low-calorie jam, try low-sugar pectins. They gel differently as pectin combines with calcium and very little sugar. The considerable amount of sugar in regular jams also acts as a preservative, to keep microorganisms from growing. Less sugar means jams and jellies spoil more easily, so consider making your low-calorie jam the freezer variety, or process it in a hot water bath.

And so the granules and powders, which we add in measured amounts and still sometimes in "pinches," quietly go about their business of creating special effects in cooking. But seldom does anyone comment on the remarkable differences they make to food. If we were to put a modern spin on the meaning of medieval alchemy, taking everyday granules and powders and transforming them into a remarkably different form that tastes incredibly good may well be alchemy at its finest.

Fascinating Flour

5

When we talk about flour, a scene that surfaces from the mirrors of our minds is driving across the Canadian prairies—big sky country. Near summer's end, at sunset, the sun looks like it's searing the horizon. Not long after, an immense prairie moon shimmers silver as it begins its evening journey. Against a spellbinding background of smoky blues and dusky golds, wild antelope graze in the wheat fields. This powerful panorama is simply there—silently affirming nature's bounty and farmers' toil. Fields of wheat, the backbone of baking, stretch as far as the eye can see.

But as always, it's the small details of the larger scene that are of practical importance. The kernels, not the fields, become the focus in cooking. Wheat is particularly important to baking because it's the only grain whose proteins form a structure strong enough to hold leavening gases for long periods—making it possible to produce a remarkable array of raised breads. While the flour, bran, or coarsely milled parts of grains other than wheat are often used in baking, it's because of the special flavors and unique textures these grains contribute to doughs, rather than their ability to form a good basic structure.

Wheat also provides starch. With its ability to swell and absorb moisture, starch is also important in baking, and working alone, it's the essence of thickening.

Wheat is important to baking because it's the only grain whose proteins form a structure strong enough to hold leavening gases for long periods.

Flour, Up Close

Think of grains of wheat as kernels of possibility. As long as their outer protective layers remain intact, wheat can be stored for years. The process of milling releases the inner components essential to baking. Knowing how to use flours appropriately helps convert all that potential to action.

Though different types of wheat have similar components, the variety, planting times, soil conditions, and climate each play a part in making some wheat, such as durum, ideal for pastas, and others, such as red spring, more useful in flours for baking.

Whole wheat flour uses all parts (95 percent) of the kernel. This may mean grinding the whole kernel or adding back bran and germ to milled flour in their original proportions. Because the oils in wheat germ can go rancid, whole wheat flour spoils more easily than other flours.

The Inner Wheat Kernel

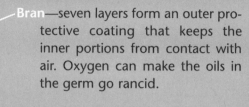

Bran—seven layers form an outer protective coating that keeps the inner portions from contact with air. Oxygen can make the oils in the germ go rancid.

Endosperm—used for white flour; contains both starch and protein.

Germ—a storehouse of nutrients for the developing plant.

Gluten Is Both Plastic and Elastic

A student in one of our classes, raised on a farm on the prairies during the 1930s, told us that as a child he used to chew kernels of wheat. As the kernels broke down and the starch was dissolved by saliva, what was left became rather elastic. "A decent sort of a substitute for kids who couldn't afford chewing gum," he allowed.

His story intrigued us. Simply by chewing, those children were developing the very factors in wheat that are essential to baking. As the children discovered, these proteins, when they are thoroughly mixed with water, have a resiliency like gum.

This elastic property in flour is essential to much of our baking because it helps hold doughs together. Envision houses under construction—some large, some small, but each needing an underlying framework. In baking, the cook creates microscopic frameworks that vary greatly in strength, from delicate cakes to sturdy yeast breads. And just as a builder uses a variety of materials to finish a house, cooks use a variety of other ingredients to finish baked products.

See for Yourself

Getting a feel for gluten

To really understand baking, take a closer look at gluten. This simple exercise shows that small differences in gluten content make big differences in the strength of a dough. You can easily isolate the gluten from cake flour, all-purpose flour, and bread flour.

Mix 1 cup (250 ml) of flour with just enough water to form a stiff dough and knead until it feels elastic. Let it rest 10 minutes. Then knead the dough while it's immersed in a bowl of cool water to wash away its starch. Change the water several times until it becomes clear.

This is gluten—the essence of flour frameworks. Feel it. Stretch it. Taste it if you like. Note the dramatic difference in the size and strength of the frameworks created by each of the flours. Form the gluten from each type of flour

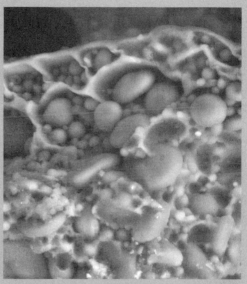

This photograph is a cross section of a bagel, magnified 1,000 times. The network of air pockets is made of gluten, which forms when two of the proteins in flour combine. Bagel dough is particularly high in gluten, which is one reason bagels are so chewy.

into a ball and bake at 350°F (180°C) until firm. The difference in the sizes of the gluten balls (resulting from the strength of the framework each forms) is even more impressive after baking.

Cook's Query

How can I find out how much protein is in my flour?

You can determine the protein content by reading the label on your bag of flour. It's usually listed as number of grams protein/100 grams flour.

The elasticity of dough comes from *gluten*, an ingredient that's crucial to most frameworks in baking. Gluten forms when liquid is added to flour and two of flour's proteins—*glutenin* and *gliaden*—form a partnership. Gluten forms a dough that is both plastic (or moldable) and elastic (or stretchable). These qualities allow doughs to rise and to hold leavening gases.

But the framework for baking isn't only gluten. If it were, your end product wouldn't be much different from the gluten balls described on page 79. While gluten often takes the leading role, it never works alone. It's always reinforced or modified by the other ingredients in a recipe. The starch granules in flour, for example, contribute to the framework by swelling as they absorb water, and then becoming rigid as moisture evaporates in the oven.

Flours by Design

Flour is milled by cleaning and grinding wheat kernels, usually sifting out the bran and germ, and then further grinding the granules to a powder. It's surprising how small flour particles become once milled. According to Harold McGee in *On Food & Cooking*, you'll be interested to know that 1 cup (250 ml) of all-purpose flour contains one hundred billion pieces of endosperm.

Part of the milling process, called *air classification*, carefully manipulates the ratio of protein to starch during milling. This

The Protein Content of Flours Determines How We Use Them

Type of Flour	Percent Protein	Uses
• Whole wheat (hard) flour	13–14 percent	All types of baking, usually in combination with all-purpose flour for yeast breads
• Bread flour	13 percent	Milled especially for yeast breads
• All-purpose flour	9–13 percent	Cookies, cakes, quick breads, and often yeast breads
• Cake and pastry flour	7.5–9 percent	Tender cakes, and pastries
• Fine cake flours	7–8 percent	Angel food cakes, fine baking
• Instant flour	2 percent	Works well in sauces and gravies, because it does not lump. Should not be substituted for all-purpose flour in baking.
• Gluten flour	40–80 percent	Added in small amounts (see page 82) to boost the protein content of low-protein flour for yeast bread

allows a miller to control the characteristics of a flour with great precision, producing flours that are suited to particular baking needs.

Once you're aware of the strength of gluten-forming proteins, the various kinds of flour on the market make sense. Bread flours are usually the highest in protein because breads need the strongest framework. Cake flours are the lowest in protein but highest in starch, since they form delicate frameworks for light and airy cakes.

Adding gluten flour is rather like boosting the octane rating in the gas for your car.

All-purpose flour is usually a blend of hard and soft wheats with often a wide variation in its protein content from brand to brand. It may also vary in strength according to where you live. So all-purpose flour in the southern United States traditionally has a lower protein content than all-purpose flour in Canada. As the name implies, all-purpose flour is intended for quick breads, cookies, and yeast breads. However, if the all-purpose flour you use has a low protein content, your bread will be more successful if you switch to bread flour, or add a little gluten flour (try 1 tablespoon per cup of flour; 15 ml per 250 ml of flour). Adding gluten flour is rather like boosting the octane rating in the gas for your car. In this case, it gives baking frameworks more power and can help you make superior breads.

Because flour looks and feels dry, people seldom think of it as containing moisture. In fact, it leaves the mill with a moisture content of about 14 percent. However, storage conditions, as well as climate, cause its moisture level to vary. Generally, the longer flour is stored, the more moisture it loses.

The next time you make pastry, take note of how much water you add. If flour has been in your kitchen for a long time or if the weather is very dry, you'll find the dough needs more water than it does if the flour has been recently purchased or if the weather is wet. Variation in the moisture content of flour is one reason baking is not precise and recipes often give a range of ingredients and baking times. It's also, we might add, one of the frustrations for beginners who feel they should follow pastry and yeast bread recipes exactly.

Flour Power

Yeast breads need a framework strong enough to hold carbon dioxide as it's slowly produced by yeast. Because each yeast cell produces only a minute amount of carbon dioxide, it takes several hours to accumulate a volume of gas with enough power to stretch the flour framework and hold it high. On a very tiny scale, this process is a perfect example of the power of collective action.

It's not just the ingredients, but also how you handle them that develops a dough's gluten potential. For a yeast bread, you need a strong flour, one that has a high protein content. This flour should be offset by only small amounts of ingredients such as fat or sugar, which interfere with gluten development. To form well-developed gluten, you must mix the dry ingredients and liquids together vigorously.

After mixing, many recipes advise you to let the dough rest for a few minutes before you begin to knead it. While this respite may

Cook's Queries

How do I make a stronger crust to hold a meat filling?

Choose a pastry recipe that contains an egg. The protein in the egg will reinforce the structure of the pastry, making it strong enough to hold a hefty filling.

Why do some pastry recipes call for vinegar?

Adding an acidic ingredient such as vinegar brings one more tenderizer into play. Acids soften gluten, breaking apart gluten strands and keeping the pastry tender.

The Art of Kneading

By kneading, you persuade a sticky dough to develop its bread-making potential. You accomplish this by repeating three simple steps and adding a little muscle power and patience.

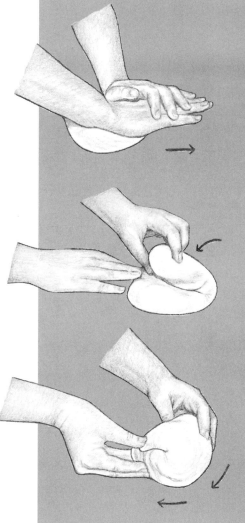

1 Begin by firmly pushing the dough away from you with the heels of your hands.

2 Then fold the dough toward you and give it a quarter turn. Let push-fold-turn become a gentle rhythm, working in additional flour slowly until the dough is no longer sticky.

3 You've done a good job when the dough starts to resist and becomes a smooth, unbroken ball with a satiny sheen.

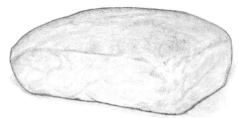

This loaf was kneaded for only five minutes.

This loaf was kneaded for 20 minutes. The loaf kneaded longer is higher and smoother because when gluten is well developed it is better able to hold gases released from fermenting yeast.

let the baker enjoy a needed cup of coffee, its primary purpose is for the benefit of the dough. Resting at this point allows moisture to disseminate evenly throughout the dough, so any dry patches disappear and all the gluten-forming proteins come in contact with moisture.

Finally, you knead the dough, a remarkable process of working and reworking the gluten until the dough is robust enough to hold the trapped gases, yet sufficiently flexible that it stretches without tearing. Kneading equalizes the temperature throughout the dough, as fermenting yeast creates heat. It also redistributes the sugar yeast requires as food, and is a huge factor in determining the texture of the finished loaf.

Kneading works in the last of the flour and turns the dough into a satiny, smooth, and resilient mass. Use the heels of your hands when kneading dough, since fingers tend to break the gluten strands. Once the dough is sufficiently kneaded, it pushes back as you push and fold.

Machines do indeed make the process of making bread easier. But if you have time, there's something very soul-satisfying about steadily kneading dough by hand for at least 10 minutes. The warmth. Its gentle rhythm. The sense of mindfulness that kneading brings. Personally, we think of this technique as a warm earthy art, as good for the kneader as it is for the rising dough.

Baker's Dough

En route to San Francisco's famed Greens Restaurant, we happened upon the San Francisco Craft and Folk Art Museum, which had a delightful exhibit on "Breads and Threads." The breads were intricate—exquisite wreaths and charming figures, all made from baker's dough. The threads, mostly embroidery, were stunningly beautiful. To our surprise, both came from schools of these crafts in Italy.

We couldn't help but think that working with baker's dough is an art that really depends on science. Salt, flour, and water in just the right proportions, and developing gluten through long and careful kneading, makes a simple dough that provides insight into how conventional doughs work. The ingredients perform the same functions in dough art as they do in baking, only in exaggerated form, to produce a hard structure that keeps for years.

For dough art, a strong gluten structure is essential, so use all-purpose flour or bread flour that contains at least 12 grams of protein per 100 grams of flour. Even extensive kneading doesn't make this dough sturdy enough, however, so you need to add salt to bring about a firming effect on the gluten.

To make your own dough art, combine 4 cups (1 liter) flour with 1 cup (250 ml) salt and gradually stir in approximately 1½ cups (375 ml) water, mixing well until the dough forms a ball. If it seems dry, add extra water (1 tablespoon/15 ml) at a time. Knead on a floured surface for 20 minutes until smooth and very elastic, then shape. Bake at 250°F (120°C) 1½ hours or until firm, lightly browned, and absolutely dry. A spray varnish reapplied each year keeps your creations well-preserved.

Use baker's dough for ornaments or festive gifts. A garlic press makes wonderful tiny curls for angels' hair or lambs' wool! Or, weave a basket using the outside of an inverted loaf pan or bowl as a form. We laugh about the bread dough basket Anne (who's not up to lambs or angels) made for Sue years ago. It looked great lined with a brightly colored napkin and filled with muffins or hot biscuits—until the day someone put it in the dishwasher!

Dough art is easy, cheap, and fun—but it's not washable! Let your imagination fly as science becomes art.

Minimizing Gluten for Tender Treats

To make yeast bread, you need gluten, but when you're making pastries, muffins, cakes, and cookies, gluten is not center stage. In these types of baking, cooks downplay gluten's strength by tenderizing doughs. One of the most effective tenderizers is fat, cut into tiny pieces for pastry, creamed for cakes, and melted for muffins. Other ingredients and techniques can also sabotage gluten's power.

Piecrusts are tricky because usually what's needed is just enough strength to hold the crust together—and no more. Therefore, each step in making shortcrust pastry is geared to minimizing gluten development.

We find pastry for pies at, or near the top, of most lists of things cooks would like to improve. Piecrusts are tricky because usually what's needed is just enough strength to hold the crust together—and no more. Therefore, each step in making shortcrust pastry is geared to minimizing gluten development.

Piecrust is less likely to be tough if you start with cake and pastry flour or an equivalent low-protein flour. Though some cooks make terrific pastry with all-purpose flour, they use extra fat to shorten a potentially stronger gluten structure.

Because fat plays a major role in making pastry both tender and flaky, the term "shortening" describes its function well. Vegetable shortening, lard, or butter are all fats that act as a barrier between water and flour. Where water can't reach flour, it interrupts the formation of gluten. The result: Gluten forms only in short strands.

To make pastry by hand, use a pastry blender to cut shortening into flour so it's the size of small peas. Some cooks prefer to add the fat in two halves. To do this, cut the first half of the shortening into very small pieces that blend with the flour, creating tenderness. Then add the second half in slightly larger pieces, building flakiness. Keep mixing to a minimum, so gluten does not develop.

If you use a food processor, freeze the fat before you add it, to offset the heat generated by the speed of processing, and blend in short pulses to keep the dough from being over-mixed.

As the pastry bakes, it becomes flaky because those little blobs of fat melt to form pockets in the dough. Moisture turns to steam, pushing apart layers of dough into the blisters that are characteristic of flaky pastry.

Some pastry recipes use oil, which acts like warm fat, coating each particle of flour so thoroughly that no gluten develops. Oil pastries are very tender, but they're mealy, rather than flaky. Often they're rolled between two sheets of waxed paper to make these fragile crusts easier to handle.

It's usually water that holds flour and fat together to form a pastry dough. Cold water keeps the shortening cold, but ice water doesn't seem to have any improved effect. Add as little water as possible! As soon as lumps of dough adhere to each other, stop. Extra liquid develops extra gluten. And too much gluten is the biggest culprit in making pastry tough. Excessive gluten also makes a sticky dough that's difficult to roll.

Cook's Query
So what does the perfect muffin look like?

A blue-ribbon winner is symmetrical with a slightly rounded top. Its surface is pebbled or bumpy. The volume of a freshly baked muffin should be about double its size as uncooked batter, and it should feel light in proportion to its size. These are indications that the leavens are well-balanced and have lifted the batter as high as possible just before it sets in the oven. A good muffin is tender and breaks apart easily. It should be slightly moist inside, with an even texture—and no tunnels!

In making successive batches of mincemeat tarts for Christmas one year, we experimented with varying amounts of water. We were amazed to find that that even an additional ½ teaspoon (3 ml) of water per cup (250 ml) of cake and pastry flour noticeably toughened the dough.

See for Yourself

Keep on stirring...

...and find out what happens if you mix a muffin batter too much. Choose a rather plain muffin recipe, without a lot of heavy grains or dried fruit, and stir the last few muffins in the batch for a few minutes longer than the rest. Notice that the longer you stir, the stringier the batter becomes. Once baked, the well-mixed muffins will probably have a pale, slick, peaked top. Break one open and chances are great you'll find tunnels inside and a compact texture. When leavening gases have to work hard to drill their way through the long gluten strands of a tough batter, they leave narrow holes that run from the bottom to the top—the hallmark of overmixing.

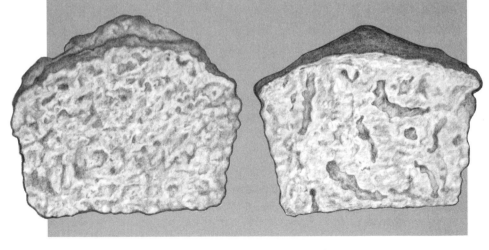

Minimal Stirring for Great Muffins

Muffins are the simplest of all baked products to make. You need just two bowls. One holds the dry ingredients, the other, the liquids. Mix wet with dry and poof—the perfect muffin. Yet muffins are frequently poorly made. Because the ratio of liquid to flour is high, it's easy to stir them too much. The more you stir, the more gluten you develop and the tougher your muffins become.

Muffins are the simplest of all baked products to make. You need just two bowls. One holds the dry ingredients, the other, the liquids. Mix wet with dry and poof—the perfect muffin.

The beauty of the muffin method is its simplicity. But the caveat to creating first-class muffins is to keep gluten development to an absolute minimum. In contrast to muffins, cakes and cookies are higher in sugar and fat. These tenderizers help keep gluten from developing. So muffins made by creaming fat and sugar may be more tender, but they're also more cakelike. You'll find variations in the muffin method, some of which have merit. Determine which you like best by trying them.

In traditional muffin-making, all the steps are geared to minimizing mixing. The fat is most often in liquid form, either melted shortening or an oil. It's usually mixed with eggs and the other liquids, then added all at once to the dry ingredients. Since fat affects tenderness, muffins with a high fat content not only taste rich, they also have a softer crumb.

Stir muffin batters only until the dry ingredients are lightly moistened. Though it may seem unusual, the batter *should* be lumpy as it's spooned into muffin pans. There may even be the odd vestige of dry flour but it will disappear as the batter bakes.

Quick breads (loaves made with baking powder and/or baking soda, along with biscuits, muffins, pancakes, and popovers) come by their name honestly. They're quickly mixed, rise promptly, and don't take long to bake. And of course, once you've learned their simple secrets, warm blueberry bran or lemon poppy seed muffins are a special treat any time.

Why Bother Creaming Shortening?

You cut fat into pastry and melt it for muffins, but in most cakes the fat is creamed. These variations in how fat is incorporated all create vastly different textures. At the same time, fat plays a crucial role in minimizing gluten development.

In conversing with the editor of a large American magazine, we discovered they stopped using the term "creaming" because, they profess, consumers no longer know what it means.

In conversing with the editor of a large American magazine, we discovered they stopped using the term "creaming" because, they profess, consumers no longer know what it means. But perhaps the problem is really that the purpose of creaming fat is seldom explained. We've talked about creaming from the perspective of sugar. Let us elaborate on what we know about well-creamed fat.

Most shortened cake recipes still call for beating together fat and sugar (alias "creaming"). This process adds air to shortened cake batters, lightening them and creating the ultimate texture of the cake.

The ease with which fat is beaten varies with the type of fat and its temperature. Most hydrogenated shortenings contain 10 to 12 percent air, deliberately incorporated to make them well-suited for creaming. Butter doesn't cream as well because it's less "plastic" or malleable at room temperature. But it adds incomparable flavor and richness that other fats can't duplicate.

A cookie is more likely to be crisp if you flatten it and grease the cookie sheet to encourage spreading. A mounded cookie is more likely to be soft.

Will That Be Soft or Crisp?

E ven business partners can't always agree on the perfect cookie. Anne likes them soft. Sue likes them crisp.

These things help make cookies SOFT

1. Remove cookies from the oven while they appear "not quite cooked." Baking for a shorter time keeps sugar in solution.

2. Include molasses, corn syrup, and honey, which have a high affinity for moisture.

3. Keep the moisture content high.

4. Use margarine and shortening; they spread less than butter.

5. Maintain an oven temperature of 375°F (190°C). Cookies brown fairly quickly, so you are likely to remove them from a hot oven sooner than if they're baked at a lower temperature.

6. Use a large amount of dough for each cookie (i.e. ¼ cup/ 50 ml) and leave it mounded on the cookie sheet.

7. Use an ungreased cookie sheet, so cookies don't spread as much. Remove to a cooling rack as soon as they are cool enough to move.

These things help make cookies CRISP

1. Bake until cookies appear done.

2. Keep the sugar content high. This ties up moisture so less is available to turn to steam. Sugar delays setting, allowing more time for the cookies to spread—larger spread makes a crisper cookie.

3. Maintain a low ratio of liquid to flour.

4. Keep the fat content high. Use butter, which tends to spread faster than shortenings.

5. Maintain an oven temperature of 350°F (180°C). This slows browning so that the cookies dry as they bake.

6. Flatten cookies or use a small amount of dough for each cookie, so they lose moisture more quickly during baking.

7. Grease the cookie sheet to encourage spreading.

Cook's Query

Why is a sauce thickened with cornstarch clear, while one thickened with flour is cloudy?

All-purpose flour is composed of both proteins and starch. Because protein has no ability to swell and doesn't participate in the thickening process, it reflects the light and makes the sauce appear cloudy. Cornstarch, on the other hand, is pure starch. Add water and heat and the starch granules will absorb water and swell. As they do so, they become transparent.

So cornstarch has twice the thickening power of flour, and because less is used, cornstarch is less likely than flour to lend a pasty taste to sauces. It's often used in fruit pies, because its transparency shows off the color of fruits well and its sheen has a 'come-hither' look that few pie fanciers can resist.

Try experimenting with other thickeners such as potato starch, for each starch makes subtle and intriguing differences to a sauce.

Mono- and diglycerides (look for them listed on shortening labels) found in most of the higher-quality shortenings make creaming easier. These are emulsifiers, which help to disperse fat particles finely throughout a batter—and interfere with gluten forming long strands.

Fats are easiest to cream and most able to trap air when they're at room temperature. But left too long in a warm kitchen or beaten too long, very soft fats act like oils. And oils don't hold air.

Once you've beaten fat until it moves easily in the mixing bowl, gradually add the sugar, while continuing to beat. Together, sugar and fat are an effective tenderizing team. This partnership also explains why cake and cookie doughs are inherently more forgiving of extra handling and mixing than pastry.

Usually after creaming fat and sugar, you add eggs, then the dry ingredients and milk or other liquid. Mix gently to blend these ingredients together. At this stage, a heavy hand can toughen the batter. It's "mixing well" at precisely the wrong time.

Starch Takes the Lead in Sauces

So far we've stressed the role of flour in baking. Flour is also a traditional thickener for sauces—a situation in which gluten takes a backseat. Here the flour's starch plays a more important role than its proteins. When flour is mixed with cold water, nothing happens. But when the mixture is heated, the starch granules in flour soften and begin to absorb liquid. Picture thousands of tiny granules swelling to form a latticework. When there's no place for any remaining liquid to flow, the sauce has thickened. Liquid is literally caught in a tender, silky trap. Cooks are the lucky recipients of this process, creating sauces that form the basis of an amazing array of dishes.

Each of the starches used for thickening has its own special properties—the way it reflects light, the temperature at which it thickens, how firmly it thickens, and if it holds its thickening power when cold or boiled or frozen. Recipes manipulate these characteristics cleverly to achieve particular results.

We realize the possibilities of the wheat kernel by sometimes emphasizing starch, sometimes working with gluten. The result? Superb sauces. Crackerjack bak-

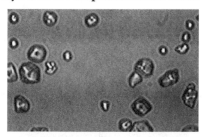
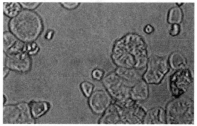
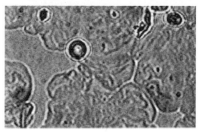

When cooked, cornstarch granules absorb liquid and swell, as these microscope images show. At 158°F (70°C), many of the granules are two or three times larger than they were at 140°F (60°C). At 194°F (90°C), the granules are ten times their original size.

ing. The old adage "practice makes perfect" would be much easier to achieve if we could just add the phrase, "and a little understanding helps."

Hooves, Fins, & Feathers

6

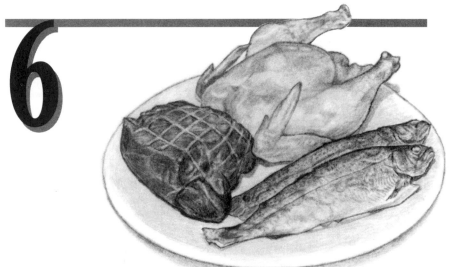

I f taste and appearance are
the only criteria for comparison, a filet of salmon, a prime rib
roast, and a chicken breast have little in common. In fact to
some cooks, our feathered, finny, and four-legged friends seem
totally unrelated—and that may be one of the reasons many
cooks have trouble cooking these foods well.

But as if peeling away another layer on an onion, inquisitive
cooks look a little deeper. If you do think about it, you realize fish,
fowl, and beef are all composed of muscle fibers, connective tissues,
and fat. The differences in how you handle these foods in cooking
depend on the way these components are arranged and distributed.

Comparing the structure of beef with that of poultry and fish
makes it easy to understand why some cuts of meat are more tender than others, why fish is prone to falling apart when cooked, and
why boiling tends to toughen, rather than tenderize, muscle tissue.

There's More to Beef Than Fat and Lean

One of the best ways to understand the relationship between muscle, fat, and connective tissue is to closely examine a piece of round steak. You'll see mostly lean, which is in fact muscle tissue, with a little fat interspersed and a layer of creamy fat around the edges. Pull the lean apart slightly with your fingers, and you'll find connective tissue—a fine, almost transparent webbing holding together bundles of tiny muscle fibers.

To some cooks, our feathered, finny, and four-legged friends seem totally unrelated—and that may be one of the reasons many cooks have trouble cooking these foods well.

If you think of the "grain" of a piece of corned beef (brisket), you'll have a good mental picture of collections of fibers forming the muscle. Much like tiny tubes, each fiber holds nutrients, juices, water, and extractives, the compounds that contribute to meat's flavor and aroma. As you might expect, the more developed the muscle fibers and the stronger the muscle, the less tender the meat.

It's not just the muscle tissues that determine tenderness, however. Connective tissue, made of proteins, also has a huge effect. Though other kinds of connective tissue may form part of less tender cuts, the most common form is collagen. When you tenderize a tougher cut of meat, such as stewing beef, you are not only breaking down muscle, you're also softening collagen. Without the tenacity of collagen, bundles of muscle fibers have little to hold them together.

Connective tissue in beef varies from barely visible membranes surrounding bundles of muscle fibers to stronger films holding one muscle to another and to even thicker webs attaching the outer surface of the meat to the surrounding fat. The greater the amount of collagen, the tougher the meat.

Fat also plays a role in tenderness. Have you ever specifically chosen a lean cut of meat, and been disappointed because it was

In this T-bone steak, you can see marbled fat interspersed throughout the muscle fibers of the red meat. Generally, a cut of meat that has a visible pattern of finely grained fat is moister and more tender than a leaner cut.

less tender and less flavorful than you anticipated? Lean meat lacks marbled fat, which plays a significant role in both adding flavor and making beef tender.

Ask your butcher to point out a top-quality T-bone or tenderloin steak and look closely at the fine tracings of fat that penetrate the lean. This is marbled fat and you'll find it only in the most tender cuts. It helps create the impression of tenderness as it melts among the muscle fibers during cooking, lubricating the meat so it's easier to chew. It also makes a major contribution to flavor as it mixes with the juices from the lean and forms complex flavor compounds as they are exposed to heat. In fact, flavor chemists have identified over 1,000 volatile compounds that come from cooked meats.

The development of muscles depends on where the muscle is located, how old the animal is, and the exercise it receives. In the wild, muscles and connective tissue develop as animals use their muscles while foraging for food and, in many cases, traveling great distances. Since there's no guarantee that wild meat comes from a young animal, meat from game is usually tougher than that of domesticated animals. In contrast to wild animals, most cattle raised for beef get little exercise, and the age at which they reach the market is carefully monitored, so they have less integral toughness.

From Antibiotics to Violin Strings

If you've ever heard someone say they "never touch beef," you might caution them to reconsider that statement. Just less than half of a carcass of beef is used for retail cuts. Canada's Beef Information Centre reports that the rest is used in an incredible variety of ways that affect most of us every day—though we seldom consider their source.

Among the edible by-products, derivatives of beef fat are used for some margarines and shortenings as well as in making chewing gums and candies.

Beef tallow provides glycerin for cosmetics and toothpaste, and is often used in soaps, cleaners, shampoos, and detergents. Some candles, automobile tires, chalk, crayons, fabric softeners, explosives, ink, and matches contain inedible fats from cattle.

The intestines form natural casings for sausages. The bones, horns, and hooves make buttons, bone china, glues, animal feeds, fertilizers, piano keys, and the nonedible gelatin that's used in making photographic film, and yes, apparently, violin strings.

The hide is tanned for leather handbags, belts, shoes, and sports equipment. Not even the hair from the hide is wasted, finding its way into such things as felt, while fine hair from the ear is used in quality paint brushes for art work.

Though biotechnology is reducing the need for animal products, beef by-products have been the source of many lifesaving and life-improving drugs, among them the insulin used by some diabetics, thrombin used to promote blood coagulation during surgery, and glucagon used to treat hypoglycemia.

In all, 99 percent of the animal is used in some way. Cattle contribute more to our daily lives than most of us realize.

Steaks and roasts from the rib and loin sections, located near the center along the back, are classed as tender. Because these aren't weight-bearing muscles, they don't develop through exercise. Cuts from these areas also have less connective tissue.

The muscles in the neck, forequarters, and lower legs (shank) get the most exercise so they are stronger and their connective tissue is more abundant. Cuts like blade, chuck, round, flank, and brisket are classified as less tender and medium tender cuts. But these cuts are also the most flavorful. As the muscles develop, they acquire more of the extractives that give meat flavor.

Cuts like blade, chuck, round, flank, and brisket are classified as less tender and medium tender cuts. But these cuts are also the most flavorful.

Before beef is sold in the marketplace, it is aged. While aging does not affect connective tissue to any great extent, the meat's own natural enzymes break down its muscle fibers, contributing to tenderness. Flavor intensifies as proteins broken down by enzymes react with sugar compounds also present in the meat. Carcasses are seldom hung (dry aging) any longer. More often "wet aging" occurs as vacuum-packed wholesale cuts of beef travel from processing plant to marketplace. Don't attempt to age your own meat. Home refrigerators are too warm, and though the enzymes that promote aging are active at kitchen refrigerator temperatures, so are spoilage bacteria.

Choosing the Cut

Choosing a cut of beef shouldn't be guesswork. Ask yourself (or your butcher), "how tender is it?" The answer will narrow your cooking choices.

If you've selected a tender cut, use dry heat—roasting, broiling, barbecuing, or pan-frying. Cooking tender meat has more to do with making it palatable by developing flavor and making it safe to

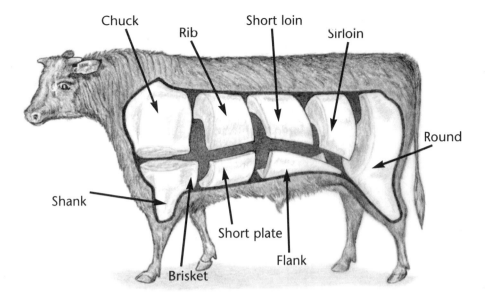

Chuck
Rib
Short loin
Sirloin
Round
Shank
Short plate
Flank
Brisket

The texture and toughness of a cut of beef depends partly on where the muscle was located on the animal's body. Meat is muscle, and the more exercise a muscle gets, the tougher it tends to be. A steer's neck, shoulders, chest, and legs get more exercise than the back muscles. That's why tender cuts come from the rib, loin, and sirloin sections.

eat than it has to do with tenderizing. The muscle tissue in tender cuts is already tender and the amount of connective tissue is minimal. So the key to keeping these meats tender is not to toughen them by overcooking.

There's little argument from chefs that tender cuts stay most tender when they're not cooked beyond the medium-rare (still pink) stage. When meat cooks longer, the protein network that forms the muscle fibers contracts both in length and width. This shrinking squeezes out juices and makes protein muscle fibers tough and dry.

Braise or stew less-tender cuts with moisture—such as broth, juices, and water. Or use the acidity of wine and beer to enhance the tenderizing effect of moisture, while combining with the meat extractives to create the rich, deep flavors of carbonades and

When Is Beef Cooked?

Ground beef should be extremely fresh and always well cooked to 160°F (71°C), since grinding exposes a huge surface area to potential bacterial growth.

Whole cuts of beef are less likely to harbor food poisoning bacteria, partly because of the sheer bulk of the muscle and partly because the skin isn't cooked (as it is with poultry). The USDA recommends that beef roasts, steaks, and chops be cooked to at least 145°F (63°C).

ragouts. Moist heat still shrinks the protein just as it does in dry heat cooking methods. But meat cooks slowly (with the lid on) in moist heat, its collagen breaks down to gelatin, and that makes the cut more tender. Think of how a stock or gravy often gels as it cools—an indicator you've been successful in transforming collagen to its more soluble form, gelatin. Less tender cuts, simmered with winter vegetables, are the basis of some of our most wonderful "comfort foods"—osso bucco, braised short ribs, and slowly simmered stews are perfect winter fare.

In addition to tenderizing tough cuts through cooking, there are several means of tenderizing meat prior to cooking it. Acids and enzymes have their limitations, but they do have a tenderizing effect. The enzymes in pineapple (*bromelain*), underripe papaya (*papain*), and kiwi (*actinidin*) act as meat tenderizers either through direct contact between the fresh fruit and the meat as it cooks, or in commercial meat tenderizers (often derived from papaya). These enzymes break down both the muscle fiber and connective tissue. Much of this action takes place as meat cooks, since the enzymes are most active between 131 and 167°F (55–75°C).

These are powerful tenderizers, as we discovered when we first tried one of our favorite curries using both chicken and fresh pineapple. We found out the hard way that you can't leave the two in each other's company for long! Bromelain breaks down already

Simmer or Boil?

S tewing that chuck? Braising a brisket? Don't let it boil! Connective tissue begins to dissolve at around 175°F (80°C) and dissolves more rapidly as the temperature rises. However, high heat shrinks muscle fibers, squeezing out juices and toughening the meat. That means meat that's cooked in moisture can still be dry. Stewing and braising are culinary balancing acts between softening the connective tissue and keeping the muscle fibers tender.

Boiling, where bubbles break the surface of a heated water-based liquid, happens at 212°F (100°C). The only way you can get water any hotter is to boil it under pressure. (As the elevation rises above sea level, the boiling point lowers roughly two degrees per 1,000 feet.)

Simmering begins at 180°F (82°C) and is characterized by bubbles rising but not breaking through the surface. We find a gentle simmer is optimal for softening connective tissue without toughening the protein in stewed and braised meat.

tender chicken, giving it a dreadfully mushy texture. Sue had better luck during a stint in Hawaii where she played with papaya and tough cuts of beef with much more pleasing results.

The leaves of the papaya also have tenderizing abilities. Food historian Waverley Root tells of tough meat being hung among the foliage of papaya trees in India and China. Is it possible, he conjectures in his classic book *Food*, that these trees can actually breathe their enzymes into the air? To our knowledge, food science hasn't looked at that one yet.

The acids in marinades work much the same way as enzymes, breaking down muscle and collagen. Marinating is most effective when meat is cut into steaks, strips, or cubes. On larger cuts, marinades have more effect on flavor than on tenderness, since the marinade can't effectively reach the inner tissues. Piercing large cuts so marinades penetrate isn't optimal either, since that allows

Cook's Queries

If veal is young beef, shouldn't it be classified as tender? Why is it usually cooked with moisture?

Veal has a high proportion of connective tissue to muscle fiber because the young animal has not had time to put on extra weight. However, because it's a young animal, veal's connective tissue is more soluble than that in beef. So cooking veal with moisture makes sense because it allows connective tissue to soften.

Why do cooks sometimes sear meat in hot fat before stewing or braising it in broth or water?

Searing meat in hot fat allows the outside to get hot enough to brown and this creates flavor. Any food cooked solely in water or broth never gets hotter than the boiling point of water—212°F (100°C) at sea level. Browning in fat allows the outside of the meat to reach much higher temperatures—usually 300 to 500°F (149–260°C). Those high temperatures quickly create intense flavors, rich brown colors, and crackling crusts. This is due to the Maillard reaction, where carbohydrates react chemically with amino compounds in proteins to create browning, deeper flavors, and tantalizing aromas.

See for Yourself

Chopping chuck

Take a piece of beef chuck—full of flavor, but not one of the tender cuts. Chop it into tiny cubes. Really tiny—this takes patience! Add water or beef broth, along with sautéed onions, garlic, paprika, and caraway seeds, and simmer gently for an hour. Notice how flavorful the soup becomes as the extractives from the meat seep into the broth. Add finely chopped tomato and a smattering of marjoram and you've got a richly flavored goulash soup. Not a stew, where meat is tenderized by moist heat, but an honest to goodness soup with richly flavored broth and tiny, tender pieces of meat. It's tender partly because the tough muscle and connective tissue have been cut so finely, and partly because your preparation allows moisture to reach and soften the connective tissue.

juices to escape and makes the meat dry. Though few would question its delectable flavor, the tender meat of sauerbraten, carefully marinated for several days, is more likely the result of long, slow cooking than it is of the marinade.

You can also tenderize tough meat by breaking down its structure through chopping, pounding, slicing, and grinding. Score a slab of flank steak with diagonal cuts and you've started a tenderizing process. It will still need moist heat and its juices will form part of the broth. Or use a sharp knife to slice a piece of round steak across the grain into razor-thin slices. Meat cut in this manner needs fast cooking at high heat so it does not dry out; stir-frying is ideal. Both will be tender, partly because muscle fibers and bands of connective tissue have been sliced into very short strands. Then there's the burger. Our most renowned North American fast food contains meat tenderized by mincing machines, which grind exercised and flavorful muscles to give us hamburger.

When we were discussing these mechanical means of tenderizing meat during a cooking class, a student once related a tale that had us all amused. In Brazil, she saw abalone, known for its inherent toughness, placed in an inner tube and repeatedly walloped against a tree trunk. Now that's pounding! We occasionally pound meat, too, to break down fibers and connective tissue for braised round steak and veal cutlets, but we use a mallet—we've never tried a tree trunk. The effect is similar, but the means not quite so dramatic.

Each of these processes, done prior to cooking, gives you the benefit of beginning with a more tender cut of meat. And who argues with a head start?

The Colors of Beef

Color is a traditional indicator of how well beef is cooked. Underlying the color of meat is the compound *myoglobin,* which contains an atom of iron, a pigment called *heme,* and a protein that coagulates easily when cooked. Myoglobin is similar to the more familiar hemoglobin, which transports oxygen in the bloodstream.

Meats with the most myoglobin are the deepest in color. Myoglobin values are .50 percent for beef, .25 percent for lamb,

Cook's Query

Why is the outside of the hamburger meat in a package bright red, but inside the meat is a dark reddish brown color?

When meat is cut and exposed to air, myoglobin picks up oxygen and becomes brighter in color. As oxygen is depleted, the color darkens. The plastic films used to package meat are often oxygen permeable, a clever means of enhancing this characteristic. This means the oxygen-rich meat on the surface of a package of fresh hamburger is a cherry red, whereas the interior is a much deeper reddish-purple.

Cook's Query

Is commercial gelatin made from meat derivatives?

The collagen in meat dissolves in moist heat to partly coagulate a broth or gravy. There's also collagen in animal bones, skin, and tendons. When concentrated, it forms a glue-like substance that is dried and marketed as gelatin in both flavored and unflavored forms. Gelatin, a protein, forms a structure that traps liquid, a characteristic important in making jelled salads and desserts. If you're looking for a vegetarian substitute, try agar-agar, made from seaweed, which is available in specialty stores and Asian markets.

and .06 percent for pork. This explains why pork is much lighter in color than beef. But meat also becomes darker as animals age, which is part of the reason that veal is paler in color than beef. As myoglobin content increases, meats darken in color.

The function of myoglobin is to hold oxygen in the muscles so it is readily available to help power muscle contractions. Those muscles that are used the most are therefore deepest in color.

Let's consider for a moment a steak sizzling on the barbecue. The outside surface browns as its proteins and carbohydrates react to the heat from the coals. Inside that steak, heat affects the structure of myoglobin causing it to change color. At a temperature of 140°F (60°C), the interior of a rare steak is still red and juicy. When beef is cooked to medium, 160°F (71°C), it changes to a pale shade of pink and meat juices become clearer. A steak cooked to the well-done stage, 170°F (77°C), is a uniform brown throughout and no longer juicy. Though color gives some visual clues to doneness, the only truly accurate way to judge how well meat is cooked is to use a meat thermometer.

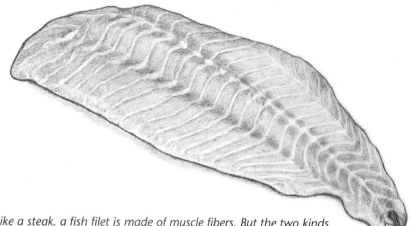

Like a steak, a fish filet is made of muscle fibers. But the two kinds of muscle have very different characteristics. The muscles of mammals and birds are made up of long fibers, gathered in bundles. The muscles of fish are made of short fibers arranged in layers, separated by sheets of thin connective tissue. Because of the short muscle fibers and weak connective tissue, cooked fish is very tender and has a tendency to fall apart.

Cooking Fish Without Fear

If you've watched an expert deftly pare a filet from the backbone of a salmon or trout, you already appreciate the delicacy of fish. If you've sautéed those filets as a last-minute entrée, you know how quickly they cook. Unlike meat, which often needs heat and moisture to tenderize it, fish is already tender. That's what makes fish cookery so simple.

Examine a filet of salmon or cod and you'll notice a distinctive ribbed appearance. Those ribs are muscle fibers lying in short, orderly layers. They're held together by a pearly webbing of connective tissue. Because this is a delicate structure, very little cooking is necessary. The biggest challenge in cooking fish is to keep it from falling apart.

Overall, fish has only a small fraction of the connective tissue that's present in meat. As you might expect, this connective tissue is more abundant in the head and tail, where there's most activity.

But the connective tissue in fish converts easily to gelatin. Though added moisture is not usually required to break the connective tissue down, you can use a little wine or broth to enhance the flavor.

If you choose rather than catch your fish, remember that selecting fish of top quality is just as important as cooking it well. Fresh fish is highly perishable. Its fat is dispersed throughout the flesh in the form of oil rather than in firm deposits as in meat. Once these oils are exposed to air, fish spoils quickly, producing off-flavors and odors. In addition, the enzymes present in fish and the bacteria that live in the gut are accustomed to functioning at cold temperatures. Refrigeration slows—but unfortunately doesn't stop—the activities that lead to deterioration, and to a fish that's past its best.

Refrigeration slows—but unfortunately doesn't stop—the activities that lead to deterioration.

One of the pleasures of West Coast living is easy access to very fresh fish. If you stand near a display of just-caught salmon at the market, the first thing you notice is that there are no fishy odors— just a whiff of the sea. And the salmon? Their eyes are clear, not

Fat or Lean?

Fatty Fish Bluefish, pompano, salmon, herring, and mackerel generally have a fat content between 6 and 20 percent. This is invisible fat in the form of unsaturated oil intermingled with the muscle tissue. If you barbecue, bake, or broil these fish, they'll baste themselves. Or pan fry them with just a little added fat.

Lean Fish Cod, flounder (sole), perch, haddock, halibut, pollack, pike, and snapper usually contain less than 5 percent fat. They are delicious, low-calorie choices, but their low fat content means you must be extra careful not to overcook them.

sunken; their flesh is firm, moist, and slightly translucent; their scales are tight and glistening. All fresh fish have these qualities. Learn to quickly bypass any seafood that doesn't meet these standards.

If you can't refrigerate fish promptly, have it packed in ice. Storage time depends on its freshness and variety, but count on two days maximum in the refrigerator. Better still, buy it (or catch it!) just before you cook it. At a memorable dinner in one of Singapore's famed East Coast seafood restaurants (their motto: "If it swims, we have it"), we began by choosing our meal from hundreds of species—all still swimming. But closer to home, bringing in the boat with freshly caught fish just before supper—and then grilling them right on the beach—is just about as fresh as you can get.

If you decide to freeze fish, don't keep it too long. Even frozen, fish doesn't last as long as beef or poultry. Use frozen, lean fish within six months and frozen fatty fish within two months.

The West Coast's reputation for seafood makes salmon one of the most popular entrées served at large gatherings. We often serve it as a treat for out-of-town guests. One of the most memorable of these feasts was an outdoor barbecue at Vancouver's spectacular Museum of Anthropology, located on a bluff overlooking the

How Long Should Fish Be Cooked?

It's hard to give a rule of thumb; there are thousands of species and many ways of cooking them. But the Canadian Department of Fisheries Guideline of cooking 10 minutes per inch (2.5 cm) measured at the thickest part, is extensively used. If fish is just out of the refrigerator, add an extra two minutes per inch. For frozen fish, double the amount of time. But you, the cook, are ultimately the best judge of when fish is done. You can always add more time, but overcooking can't be corrected.

The Lemon Slice in the Finger Bowl

t's no accident that lemon juice has long been partnered with fish. The citric acid in lemon combines with the *amines* or flavor compounds in fish, diminishing fishy odors. That's why wine, lemon, or vinegar are traditionally part of a court bouillon for poaching, why a wedge of lemon often accompanies fish dishes, and why the slice of lemon in the finger bowl keeps your fingers smelling fresh.

Pacific Ocean, the offshore islands, and, in the distance, mountains that are snow-capped even in summer. Filets of salmon were cooked on huge grills, under the watchful eyes of towering totem poles, the quiet guardians of indigenous peoples' lore and wisdom. Such an inspiring setting makes those of us who live here very conscious of our good fortune in having access to such treasures from the sea. And it underscores the need to take care of these limited resources. For this reason, we believe that using fish wisely includes cooking it perfectly—and savoring each mouthful.

When you cook fish, proteins in the muscle fibers coagulate, and collagen softens and turns to gelatin just as in cooking beef. The temperature at which this happens, however, is much lower for fish than for meat. So fish cooks very quickly.

To minimize moisture loss, grilling, baking, or sautéing fish uses a relatively high heat for a short time. When you are poaching fish, begin with a cold liquid and bring it just to simmering

Cooked fish flakes apart easily when prodded with a knife. Cook a fish until it's almost done in the center and let the residual heat cook it the rest of the way.

temperature for maximum flavor and moistness. If the poaching liquid is bubbling, a delicate fish can literally disintegrate as the liquid dissolves its collagen. This is why some cooks choose to wrap fish in cheesecloth before poaching, making it easier to lift without breaking once it's cooked. Or you can wrap the fish in parchment with a little wine or broth and allow steam to cook it quickly.

When *you are poaching fish, begin with a cold liquid and bring it just to simmering temperature for maximum flavor and moistness.*

No matter which method you use, watch for these signs of doneness. Your first indicator is that the flesh loses its translucent sheen and becomes opaque. Prod its layers gently with a knife. You'll find cooked fish separates easily into flakes as its connective tissue dissolves and there's nothing to hold muscle fibers together. Cook fish just until it's almost done in the center. Undercooking is a safer bet than overcooking. Residual heat continues the cooking process even after the fish is removed from the heat. It's no problem to add a few extra minutes, but it's impossible to rectify if the fish is overdone. Serve immediately—fish isn't gracious about waiting.

Cooking fish too long overcoagulates the proteins in the muscle tissue, so they toughen and shrink. As with meat, that squeezes out juices and flavor, leaving the fish dry and chewy. Overcooked fish is also prone to falling apart.

One of our favorite bastes for low-fat fish is a simple mixture of mayonnaise, a touch of honey, and a dash of soy sauce. Spread it on top of a halibut steak, sprinkle with some freshly chopped herbs, and bake or barbecue it. There's no need to turn it over on the grill; heat travels quickly through fish and the creamy basting sauce keeps it moist. Or top it with a pat of butter mixed with chopped fresh herbs (dill is one of our favorites) as soon as it's done.

Marinades are often used with fish to prevent drying, as well as to add flavor. But since fish is already tender, don't marinate it for long or the acids in the marinade will actually do the cooking for you. This is the basis of fish dishes like ceviche, which are marinated but not cooked before serving.

A Primer on Poultry

When you consider muscle, fat, and connective tissue with respect to poultry, it's like having the best of both worlds. The more developed muscle tissues with their fat and flavor extractives are found in the darker meat of a bird. And as an added bonus, there's the delicate meat of the breast. One is so different from the other that on a large bird, such as a turkey, you're often asked which you prefer—dark meat or white?

Breast meat in poultry is composed of short muscle fibers. Because domesticated birds seldom fly, their chest muscles get little exercise. So the breast does not develop as many flavor extractives and has less connective tissue, therefore it's more delicate in flavor, easier to digest, and cooks more quickly than dark meat.

Less fat, however, means breast meat is also prone to becoming dry during cooking, whereas dark meat stays lubricated and moist.

Whether a chicken part is dark or light depends on how much myoglobin the muscle contains. Myoglobin is a pigment that stores oxygen. Muscles that get frequent and strenuous exercise need more oxygen and have more myoglobin, which makes the meat darker. Since domestic chickens spend a lot of time standing and walking but rarely fly, their leg meat is dark and their breast meat is light.

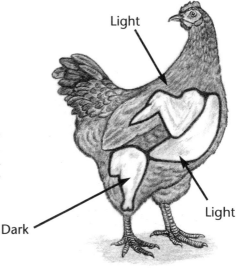

Light

Light

Dark

But because the darker portions contain more connective tissue, the key to cooking them well is either careful basting to hold moisture inside the meat, or moist heat to transform connective tissues to gelatin.

Broth or wine seems to benefit both parts. It keeps the white parts moist, adds flavor, and makes the darker parts tender as it breaks down collagen. So many recipes for poultry include some moisture. Poultry's mild flavor also marries well with herbs and spices, making it highly adaptable to the recipes of many different cultures.

Most Poultry Is Tender

Chicken is generally marketed by age and often its label indicates an appropriate cooking method. Broilers, fryers, roasters, capons, and Rock Cornish game hens are all tender, so you can cook them by roasting, baking, broiling, or frying—the same dry heat methods used for tender beef.

In fact, most chicken on the market is tender, so you seldom have to worry about tenderizing. As with fish, the biggest concern is to avoid overcooking.

Stewing chicken or fowl are older and have had more exercise along the way. Like the tougher cuts of beef, these are best cooked slowly with gentle, moist heat to break down more developed muscle and tougher connective tissue. They are, however, full of flavor and great for stock. Or, when well-simmered, they make a fine chicken pot pie or soup.

Fresh poultry is highly perishable and so is best used or frozen within two days after purchasing. Immediately before cooking, wash it in cold running water and pat it dry with paper towels.

Poultry is more prone to spoilage than other meats because it is usually sold and cooked with the skin on, and that's where the bacteria collect. Cooking to the well-done stage (180°F/82°C) is your insurance that harmful microorganisms are killed through cooking. Once cooked, however, you still have to remember that the danger zone for microbial growth lies between 40 and 140°F (5–60°C). Keep poultry either hot or well-chilled.

When Is Poultry Done?

The best way to eliminate the guesswork is to use a meat thermometer, particularly with larger cuts and whole birds. Place the thermometer so the bulb is in the thickest part of the thigh, the largest muscle. Make sure it isn't touching the bone, which conducts heat differently and will register a lower temperature than the muscle.

When you cook a stuffed bird, the temperature in the thigh should reach 180°F (82°C). At that temperature, the stuffing should measure 165°F (74°C), rendering it safe to eat. Cook unstuffed poultry to 170°F (77°C). As with any large piece of meat, remember that cooking continues after it's removed from the oven, so take a whole turkey from the oven when the thermometer is a few degrees shy of the desired final temperature—and let the bird stand for a few minutes. This completes the cooking, allows the juices to settle, and makes carving easier.

In the absence of a thermometer, or with smaller pieces like breasts, legs, and thighs, make a tiny slit in the meat with the tip of a sharp knife. The juices should run clear, not pink. It's important to cook poultry adequately, without overcooking. When it's overdone, poultry behaves in the same way as overcooked beef or fish, becoming dry and somewhat stringy.

A vendor in Vancouver's colorful, oceanside market sells nothing but poultry. His display cases are tiered with plump roasting chickens, perfect little Rock Cornish game hens, and moist, supple turkey breasts—all nestled on ice. His business is booming. No doubt that has a lot to do with the fact that poultry is so versatile. It sits quite

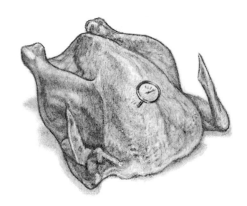

A meat thermometer eliminates guesswork when you are trying to determine whether poultry is fully cooked.

deservedly in two very different dining categories—"dinner in 15 minutes" and "potentially elegant."

You can't beat quickly sautéed chicken tenders (the small filet under the breast) for a fast fajita dinner. Roll them in a soft tortilla with chopped tomato, onion, and peppers, peanut sauce, and a little mayo and yogurt blended with garlic. On the other hand, chicken breasts stuffed with asiago and goat cheeses, fresh herbs, and chopped, toasted hazelnuts, topped with warm beurre blanc, is a very classy entrée.

In spite of their individuality, beef, fish, and poultry have a lot in common.

Many of us enjoy beef, fish, and poultry because each adds its own distinctive dash to dinner. Yet, in spite of their individuality, beef, fish, and poultry also have a lot in common. All are muscle fibers made of protein, held together by forms of connective tissue and soothed and softened by fats and moisture. The next time you're browsing through your recipe books, think about these elements and how each affects tenderness. The incredible number of ways cooks have devised to work with these basics is truly astounding.

Cook's Queries

Why are whole chicken and turkey timed with a roasting chart rather than on a minutes-per-pound basis like beef?

A small bird has a larger proportion of bone to meat than a heavier bird. Heat takes longer to travel through bone than it does muscle. Therefore, small birds take more cooking per pound than larger ones. And even small birds require a significant amount of heat to begin lifting their temperature from refrigeration point to desired doneness.

Once heating begins, a bird's mass helps facilitate cooking as heat moves from fiber to fiber through the muscle tissues. For these reasons, a 10-pound (4.5 kg) turkey takes approximately 3½ hours, while a 25-pound (11.4 kg) turkey takes roughly five hours.

What causes a dark red color in the meat next to the bones of cooked chicken?

This discoloration is due to pigments in hemoglobin being released from the bone as the meat cooks. Usually it happens in poultry that's been frozen and defrosted before cooking. It's prevalent in young chickens (broilers and fryers) because their bones are porous. Though it may look a bit strange, the meat is safe to eat.

Focusing on Flavors

The cooking is finished. The table's set. Bon appétit! You're about to enjoy grilled halibut with mango-tomato salsa, tiny red potatoes, and the first asparagus of the season. But as you take that first bite, here's a question to contemplate.

Lip-smacking salsa and halibut so fresh it still smells of the sea. What exactly is it that makes this meal taste so good? That may seem like a simple question, yet it's really one of the most complex dimensions of cooking.

Before we consider the chemistry of tastes and smells, you might think about how your body detects the flavors and aromas of the meal you've just prepared. First, volatile compounds from the food float through the air from the torn leaves of the cilantro and the chopped mango in the salsa to reach the olfactory receptors of your nose. When you take that first bite of grilled halibut and begin to break it down by chewing, other flavors are released and then enhanced as the warmth of your mouth makes them more volatile.

Quickly, your senses are assaulted by a myriad of changing signals. The taste buds in your mouth, the olfactory receptors of your nose, and the tactile sensors of your mouth and tongue send the signals to your brain, which evaluates the combined sensations to decide whether this bite of food tastes good or not. As you might imagine, scientists are still unscrambling the intricate processes by which familiar flavors are coded in the brain and remembered.

The Basic Tastes

Traditionally, scientific discussions about flavor begin with four basic tastes—sweet, salty, sour, and bitter. In recent years, researchers in flavor chemistry have added the concept of umami (see page 120). There is also ongoing debate among academics as to whether the concept of only four primary tastes meets the needs of contemporary science and industry.

You may have heard that the sensations of the four basic tastes are localized on specific areas of the tongue: sweetness could be sensed at the tip, salty and sour at the sides, and bitter at the rear.

Traditionally, scientific discussions about flavor begin with four basic tastes—sweet, salty, sour, and bitter. In recent years, researchers in flavor chemistry have added the concept of umami.

Scientists now believe that sensitivity to the four basic tastes is not limited to specific tongue locations. Taste receptor cells are also found on the soft palate, cheeks, and esophagus. Apparently, children have more receptor cells than adults in these particular areas.

That mango salsa and grilled halibut—and most foods you serve—are never the carriers of single taste; their flavors are a mix-

Umami

Some 1,200 years ago, Japanese cooks identified a flavor that they called *umami*. This Japanese word, pronounced "oo-mommy," hadn't made it into Webster's dictionary when this book went to press, but flavor chemists use it to refer to a fifth taste, distinct from the other basic tastes.

This flavor is an elusive one. Even Japanese culinary experts can't seem to agree on an exact definition for umami. It's been described by some as a savory characteristic or the quality of deliciousness, but apparently every expert you ask has a slightly different take on the word.

At the turn of the century, scientists identified some of the compounds that are responsible for this difficult-to-define flavor. While the compounds that provide umami have little taste or flavor on their own, they have been found to enhance the natural flavors of the foods to which they are added.

One of the umami-taste compounds is *glutamate* or *glutamic acid,* one of the most common amino acids found in nature. Amino acids are the building blocks of proteins. When glutamic acid is not bound together with other amino acids in proteins, it gives food the distinctive umami taste. Unbound or "free" glutamic acid is responsible, in part, for the flavor-enhancing characteristics of tomatoes, certain cheeses, soy sauce, and other fermented protein products.

Monosodium glutamate (MSG) is the sodium salt of glutamic acid, and adding MSG to foods increases their glutamate content. When added to meat broth, for instance, MSG increases the overall taste intensity and makes the broth taste meatier. In 1992, the International Food Information Council sponsored a workshop at which food editors were asked to identify and describe the umami taste after tasting samples of chicken broth. The editors described the broth containing MSG as "rich," "well-rounded," "savory," "full-bodied," and "more chicken-like."

In the 1960s, MSG was reported to be responsible for a collection of symptoms dubbed "Chinese Restaurant Syndrome." These symptoms include numbness at the back of the neck and a feeling of pressure in the chest and face. Over the years, MSG has been one of the most intensely studied food additives, and subsequent scientific studies failed to link these symptoms with MSG. As a result of these studies, MSG has been designated as safe by the American Medical Association's Council on Scientific Affairs, the National Academy of Sciences, and the U.S. Food and Drug Administration.

ture of the basic four. Your perception of these tastes is also affected by the food's aroma, its texture, and its appearance. Even if we ignore these factors, we need to consider how the basic tastes interact—one may alter the perceived intensity of another, so that even the fundamental components become tangled. Here's a little of what we know about the chemical compounds responsible for the basic tastes and how they affect each other.

Sweet

Since sugars are the main source of sweetness in food, they have become the standard by which sweet flavor perception is measured. The flavor of sugar is unique in that it imparts pure sweetness without aftertaste, but alcohols, their related aldehydes, some amino acids, and glycerol also add sweetness to food.

Generally, but not always, sugar makes sour foods seem less sour. So it makes sense that the tartness of lemon is offset with sugar in many refreshing desserts and hot weather thirst quenchers. Sugar's effect on acidic or sour foods is probably the reason that our grandfather used to sprinkle sugar on freshly sliced tomatoes. In his day, the most popular varieties of homegrown tomatoes were more acidic than they are today.

Small amounts of sugar added to salty solutions have been found to reduce the salty taste. That's probably why some people advise adding sugar to counteract too much salt in a stew or casserole.

A touch of sweetness can also enhance other flavors. A sprinkling of sugar added to the cooking water for corn, carrots, or peas minimizes their starchy or earthy notes, and highlights the sweet flavors of young vegetables. The presence of natural sugars in fruits and vegetables enhances their aroma and also contributes to their flavor. Indeed, sweetness is one thing that differentiates fruits from vegetables, with fruits having higher concentrations of both sugars and volatile oils.

Though most people like sweets, a dessert that's only sweet is unappealing. But sweetness tickles the taste buds when balanced by fruits that are acidic, playing sweet against sour—as in strawberry shortcake, the famous Pavlova meringue with kiwi and raspberry, or that sour lemon tart recipe we are still trying to perfect.

Salty

The saltiness of table salt (sodium chloride) is attributed to sodium; the chloride portion of the salt molecule has no apparent taste of its own. Scientists believe that sodium fine-tunes your body's taste mechanisms because it is a major component of the electrical currents in most nerve cells. Adding a small amount of sodium to food tends to stimulate the electrical responses of the taste cells, which may underlie the mechanisms through which salt is known to enhance flavors.

It's been found that, in general, salts and acids enhance each other at moderate concentrations. However, at higher concentrations, such as in pickles, they appear to suppress each other. Salt has also been found to increase perceptions of sweetness. This may explain why some folks put salt on cantaloupe or grapefruit.

Studies also consistently show that sodium salts (which for cooks means common table salt) suppress bitter flavors. So in addition to drawing forth water from bitter eggplants or cucumbers, salty tastes mask the bitter ones. Salt's effect on bitterness may also be why some people add a little salt to coffee grounds before the coffee brews. (But the question always niggles at us: What prompted anyone to do this in the first place?)

Sour

Sour sensations are associated with acids, which are present in ingredients like vinegar and wine, and in acid salts, like cream of tartar. Many organic acids contribute to the distinctive flavors of fruits and vegetables. These can break down during cooking and change to other acids. This, in part, may be why cooked apples are less tart than raw apples. Some volatile acids evaporate with the steam of cooking; others remain in the cooking water.

And it's always interesting to note that the degree of sourness of a solution does not necessarily correspond to its acidity. The juice of a white grapefruit has the same acidity as that of a ruby red grapefruit, but the ruby red juice tastes much sweeter.

It has recently been found that citric acid and sugar (sucrose) help reduce the burn of hot peppers and the pungency of black pepper. Just after reading about this, we enjoyed a pungent Indian vegetable curry and couldn't help but notice how the sweet-tasting lemon-and-yogurt condiment served with it reduced its fire to a smolder in a most refreshing manner.

Bitter

Of the four basic tastes, people can detect bitterness most easily. In fruits and vegetables, bitter compounds are part of nature's repertoire of protective devices, designed to keep predators away. Quinine, the compound that lends tonic water its pungent qualities, is the accepted standard for bitter taste, because it can be detected at a

Vanilla—Artificial or Real?

When you sniff a bottle of pure vanilla extract, you're inhaling exotic chemicals that originated inside a long narrow vanilla bean, the fruit of a giant orchid that bloomed in Madagascar or Mexico or the Caribbean. When harvested, that vanilla bean was totally devoid of flavor. Its heady aroma and richness developed because of the action of enzymes during fermentation and the traditionally lengthy curing. (Some companies are currently working on a rapid curing process that also enhances the flavor.)

Vanilla's flavor is formed by 250 volatile substances, the most predominant being *vanillin*. The process of transforming beans to vanilla extract is complex and includes curing the beans, crushing them, and steeping them in alcohol. No wonder real vanilla is costly.

Artificial vanilla is made from vanillin, a simple chemical and the first flavor compound to be synthesized. For many years, its source was *eugenol* from the oil of cloves. Today, vanillin is most frequently obtained as a by-product of pulp in paper manufacturing. The flavor of artificial vanilla lacks the complexity of its real counterpart, though its light odor is similar.

threshold as low as 10 ppm (parts per million).

Though you may not commonly use the term alkaloids, you're probably familiar with a number of bitter compounds like caffeine and *theobromine* (both of which are found in tea, coffee, cocoa, and cola). There are other bitter agents, too. Among them are *limonin* and *naringen*, constituents in grapefruit and oranges. Occasionally, bitter notes appear in avocados, and the particular chemicals contributing to this characteristic have been isolated by scientists in the seed, flesh, and skin of the immature fruit. Sometimes bitterness is caused by the breakdown of molecules, such as the particular proteins in cheese that can lend cured cheeses an undesirable tone.

Taste Sensations

Adding to the complexity of flavor are taste sensations. These aren't really tastes, but they can augment flavor and have a powerful effect on your perception of food. Maybe you know someone who likes cold pizza for breakfast—or someone who can't abide the thought of cold pizza. The temperature of a food is one important taste sensation. Frozen foods often require a higher level of seasoning, both because the volatile compounds responsible for aroma are more sluggish at cold temperatures, and because very cold substances can anesthetize the taste buds, dulling your sense of taste. Sherbet, which melts very quickly on a hot day, tastes sweeter in its melted form than in its frozen state.

Taste sensations have a powerful effect on your perception of food. Maybe you know someone who likes cold pizza for breakfast—or someone who can't abide the thought of cold pizza.

In contrast, salted foods taste saltier when cold. So if you're cooking food to be served cold, don't adjust the salt levels while it's still hot.

Serving food very hot can also modify how its flavor is perceived. Taste sensations are reduced if the temperature of the food is above 86°F (30°C). You may not notice the bitter tones in your mug of hot coffee, but as it cools its bitterness becomes more noticeable.

Texture is another important factor affecting flavor. Grainy, brittle, smooth, chewy—these are all characteristic textures describing how a bite of food feels in your mouth. Anne's family much

Fooling the Senses About Flavors

Research has shown that people have a hard time identifying flavors in colored jellies when the color of the jelly is inconsistent with the flavor. Given identically flavored puddings in a taste test, participants perceived the darker-colored pudding to be stronger in flavor. What's the bottom line? Color significantly affects your perception of flavor. That explains why professional tasters often perform their tasks in booths where red light masks the true colors of the foods they are tasting.

prefers a favorite cheddar cheese, dill, and potato soup served chunky-style rather than smooth. In fact, no one in the family likes it when it's pureed in the blender, even though the ingredients are identical. You can probably think of many examples in your own repertoire of meals where you prefer one texture over another. Jam versus jelly? Peanut butter that's chunky or smooth?

Two taste sensations you may be less familiar with are *astringency* and *pungency.* Astringency is noticed as a dry, puckery feeling in the mucous membranes lining the mouth, caused by the reaction between compounds called *tannins* or *polyphenols* with the protein in your saliva. Astringency is often associated with bitterness, as many polyphenols and tannins also create bitter taste sensations.

Astringent properties can be unpleasant, as they are in unripe bananas or poor wine. However, an astringent note can also be appealing, as it sometimes is in a cup of hot tea. For those who prefer a milder flavor, the astringency of tea can be tempered by adding milk or cream. The proteins in the milk or cream remove tea's astringent qualities by binding with the polyphenols so they become inactive.

Pungency relates to the characteristic hot, sharp, and stinging sensations found in chili peppers, fresh garlic, and watercress. Sometimes volatile aromatic compounds warn us of a pungent

Cook's Query
What puts the fire in peppers?

Take a moment to recall your last encounter with hot food. A mild tingle? Or did it hit you with an eye-watering, throat-searing burn? That wallop is caused by alkaloids, the most common of which is *capsaicin* (pronounced kap-SAY-ih-sin). Capsaicin in all its different forms is strictly heat. On its own, it has virtually no flavor or odor. It stimulates the pain receptors in the mouth, boosting body temperature and adrenalin level. Eating peppers can simulate the same reactions you experience in bungee jumping, white-water rafting, or other on-the-edge sports. We recommend the peppers as being safer and cheaper, but still fun!

Capsaicin is manufactured by glands of the placenta (the fleshy white spongy core) at the base of the ribs inside the pepper. The seeds are not the source of heat. Any heat in the seeds has been picked up by their close contact with the inside ribs. So you can adjust the heat in your chile rellenos or Mexican mole by including or discarding the inner portions of the pepper.

The degree of heat in peppers has actually been measured and documented. The Scoville Scale rates mild bell peppers at 0 Scoville Heat Units; poblanos at 1,000 to 1,500; jalapeño peppers between 2,500 and 5,000; cayenne at 30,000 to 50,000; and the torrid habanero at a whopping 100,000 to 300,000 Scoville Heat Units. Of course, the heat also varies within each variety according to the growing season, the garden, and the particular plant. And mature peppers are much more pungent than immature ones.

When cooking with peppers, don't confuse hotness with flavor. Flavor is concentrated in a pepper's fleshy outer tissue and is generally linked to color. The stronger the color, the fuller the flavor.

The difference in flavors created by roasting versus boiling vegetables can be quite dramatic. Try roasting a mixture of vegetables, such as peeled sweet potatoes, turnips, parsnips, and onions. Cut in pieces about the same size and brush each lightly with olive oil. Season with salt and pepper. Roast for 90 minutes at 375°F (190°C), turning the vegetables occasionally. About halfway through cooking, add large slices of red and green pepper and several whole cloves of peeled garlic (again, lightly oiled). Compare the flavors and aromas that develop as the vegetables roast with those of similar vegetables that have been cooked quickly in water. Notice how roasted vegetables have deeper, richer tones and colors as the higher temperature and extended cooking time promote the creation and release of flavors and aromas. As moisture evaporates, the flavors are further concentrated and amplified.

flavor—when you chop a clove of garlic, for example, the aroma that assaults your nose gives warning that you're in for blockbuster flavor. But other pungent foods—such as ginger, black pepper, and chili peppers—have very few volatile compounds. As a result, your nose gets no hint of what's to come and these foods catch you by surprise as you take that first unsuspecting bite. Instantly, your whole mouth is assaulted by the searing heat of *capsaicinoids* (found in chilis), *gingerols* (found in fresh young ginger and transformed into even more potent compounds as ginger ages), or *piperine* (the pungent compound in peppercorns).

The Importance of Aroma

Imagine the smell of an apple pie baking in the oven. The aroma of a food contributes significantly to its flavor. You've probably heard that if you pinch your nose, a bit of apple and a bit of potato taste the same. And you may recall how little pleasure there is in eating when you have a bad cold. This is because your taste system can only detect the four basic tastes; you rely on your nose for the rest. In fact, most of what we call flavor is really odor, as the olfactory system is 10,000 times more sensitive than the ability to taste.

You've probably heard that if you pinch your nose, a bit of apple and a bit of potato taste the same.

When you smell the welcome aromas of dinner, airborne molecules rush through your nostrils and onto the roof of your nasal cavity. There they bind with smell receptor sites creating odor signals that are picked up by nerve endings and transferred to the olfactory bulb in your brain. And as food releases its volatile molecules, they travel from the back of your mouth into your upper nasal cavity, so that the majority of what you perceive as taste is really due to your ability to smell. The number of olfactory receptors in the nose is estimated to number in the order of 100 million. The olfactory nerve cells are the only nerve endings in the body that are exposed, and they constantly replace themselves—an indicator of the importance of the sense of smell.

Here's an example of the sensitivity of the olfactory system. One of the primary components of potato scent is *methionine*. In a lab, researchers simmered a solution of methionine, and folks walking into the lab commented on the pleasant potato smell. Then the researchers set up two saucepans—one with a solution of methionine and the other with boiling potatoes. People could easily distinguish the real thing by smell—a tribute to the power of the human nose and the complexity of flavor chemistry. The scent of a boiling potato is made up of a complex array of volatile compounds.

Your Perceptions of Flavor Change

People vary widely in their abilities to detect aromas. One research project noted a 39,000-fold difference among 78 people in detecting an aromatic compound. It seems that variable sensitivity might help explain food preferences. But food preferences also change, not just from one person to another, but in a given individual. When you're hungry, the smell of food can be appealing; when you're not, the same smell may be less pleasant.

At different times in your life, too, you may find your food preferences alter. Studies show a decline in sensitivity to some odors (and therefore flavors) as we reach our forties, to most odors in our sixties, and to almost all odors in our eighties. There is a bigger decline in our sense of smell than in our ability to taste as we age. One theory suggests that as people age, olfactory cells are gradually replaced by cells that have no ability to detect odors, lessening the sensitivity to flavors. Another explanation may be that the nose is more vulnerable than the mouth to the ravages of daily life, such as pollution and infections.

Traumatic events can also affect your perception of flavors. Having suffered a severe head injury, a friend finds the taste of chocolate repugnant—a flavor he formerly loved. The ability to smell is jeopardized in roughly 6 percent of people who receive head injuries.

Creating Flavors Through Cooking

One of the main reasons that you cook food is to make it taste better. Through chemical reactions, you intensify the flavor of foods by producing volatile compounds that aren't present in the uncooked foods. Heating foods of different chemical compositions together creates an astronomical variety of volatile flavor compounds.

As a cook, you are probably aware that many steps involved in cooking change, or enhance, the way food tastes and smells. For example, chemical reactions that cause food to brown—logically known as "browning reactions"—are responsible for the distinctive flavors of roasted coffee beans; maple syrup (which is boiled from sap); toasted bread, nuts, and coconut; dry roasted spices; and flour browned for a roux.

The temperature at which food cooks also affects its flavor. When foods cook in water, they never get hotter than the boiling point of water. Quite different flavors develop in baking, roasting, frying, or broiling where parts of the food reach appreciably higher temperatures. Even when cooking has finished, the temperature to which the food has been raised, its degree of doneness, and amount of waiting time all affect the flavors and aromas that develop.

Maple syrup, coffee beans, and toast all get some of their flavor from the same chemical reactions that turn them brown.

Creating Flavors Through Fermentation

Heat is just one way to develop flavor. Fermentation, in which sugars are broken down by bacterial action or yeast enzymes to form acids, is also responsible for an incredible array of flavors and textures. Fermentation is part of the process by which milk changes to yogurt, buttermilk, and cheese; and cabbage and cucumbers become sauerkraut and dill pickles. Kimchee, the pungent Korean pickle with its pervasive odor, is fermented from cabbage. The strongly flavored fish sauces of Thailand and Vietnam take a year to cure as layered fish and salt are transformed to a clear, amber-colored sauce. Soy sauce made from soybeans mixed with roasted grain—usually wheat, sometimes barley or rice—is injected with a yeast mold and fermented for months or even years.

Using Spices and Herbs

Perhaps the most obvious way to make a dish more flavorful is to add spices and herbs—like magic wands in the hands of a clever cook. Threads of saffron weave heady carpets of flavor and aroma. A few sprigs of fresh rosemary speak of earthiness, freshness, and pungency. Often the use of special seasonings is so ingrained in ethnic dishes that where or when they were first introduced remains part of their allure. Consider a seasoning as simple as the cinnamon used in Greek moussaka—a delightful addition, but where did it originate? Or the Syrian spice mix, baharatm, which flavors ground meats and stews; its precise mixture varies according to who's cooking. Yet science has unraveled some of the mystery of seasonings in food.

Herbs, usually the leaves of plants with a distinctive aromatic character, often have relatively low levels of essential oils. Fresh herbs can differ markedly from dried ones because their flavors alter during drying and storing.

Some flavor chemists group herbs according to the main flavor component of their essential oils—which does not necessarily correspond to their botanical classification. Herbs that are by custom used together often have similar sensory effects. When blended, not only do they reinforce each other in terms of their major flavor components, but they also complement each other in their minor nuances. For example, herbs such as bay laurel (*Lauraceae* family), rosemary (*Labiatae* family), and Spanish sage (*Labiatae* family), all contain *cineole,* often described as eucalyptus-like or fresh with a penetrating odor. These herbs have a bitter afternote that plays nicely against the delicate, sweet flavors of fish, veal, pork, or chicken.

Sweet basil, marjoram, and tarragon have alcohols and various esters in their essential oils. Words such as "green and herbaceous, with a hint of balsamic, floral notes" describe their aroma. Consider how sweet basil complements sliced ripe tomatoes, or imagine the whiff and flavor of fresh tarragon butter as it melts on a barbecued chicken breast. Though each of these so-called "sweet herbs" has a distinctive flavor profile, they're also used for blended seasonings because both their flavors and odors are considered to be well-rounded.

The spicy and aromatic herbs—thyme, oregano, and savory—all contain *thymol* and/or *carvacrol*. Their odor can be sharp and adds a woodsy, richly herbaceous note to foods.

Greek and dalmatian sages (also of the *Labiatae* family) contain *thujone,* mellowed by cineole, making them a powerful and effective seasoning. Their stern character percolates right through stuffings and into the muscle tissue of poultry. Sage also holds its own when used with the more assertive flavors of game.

In contrast to herbs, spices are most often from the fruits, seeds, bark, and flowers of plants—parts that are highly aromatic. Typically of tropical or semitropical origin, most spices contain a relatively high percentage of volatile oils, as well as nonvolatile components that hold flavors or color. Generally, the flavors of spices are much more powerful than those of herbs. For instance, on an index classifying flavoring strength, chervil (rated at 45) has the lowest flavor impact among the herbs and sweet bay leaves (rated 140) have the highest. Among spices, however, sweet paprika (registering at 50) has the lowest impact, but mace stands at 340, turmeric at 400, cloves at 560; chilies ring in at 1,000.

So the divergency in flavor impact among the seasonings ranges from a whisper to a scream. It speaks of the wisdom of seasoning judiciously, and of highlighting rather than overpowering the flavor of the foods you prepare.

Creating flavors poses a two-pronged challenge. On the one hand, you unconsciously (as well as deliberately) develop flavors in foods as you cook. On the other, the flavors you create will be interpreted differently by each guest at your table. Being sensitive to both aspects of flavor adds a new dimension to your cooking. Eating becomes more pleasurable and also more intriguing.

Ground spices lose their characteristic aromas and flavors more quickly than whole spices. That's because grinding exposes the flavorful oils to the air, allowing them to evaporate.

Making Changes

8

As you lift the main course from the oven and put the last minute touches on the salad, you've probably just run through many of the processes discussed in the preceding chapters.

Take a moment to marvel at the changes that have taken place in the food and remember that science is quietly involved as you prepare even a simple meal.

But your exploration of science and food doesn't need to end once you've served the meal. If a dish hasn't turned out quite as you expected, try to figure out why, keeping in mind that errors are sometimes the fault of the recipe, rather than the cook. Consider the changes you might make for next time and write them down. We urge you to view mistakes as opportunities for learning—and always try again.

Some cooking mistakes encourage more rapid learning than others. Consider the flaming Christmas pudding that we mentioned in chapter 1, the one that left Sue with singed eyebrows. A little less eyebrow was a conspicuous trigger for learning. At the time, we didn't realize that the boiling point of alcohol (175°F/80°C at sea level) was so much lower than that of water. But we learned (the hard way) that merely waving a flame near the fumes of warmed, evaporating alcohol was enough to ignite it instantly. The higher the proof, the more easily alcohol ignites. Perhaps Sue was lucky only her eyebrows were sacrificed.

The higher the proof, the more easily alcohol ignites. Perhaps Sue was lucky only her eyebrows were sacrificed.

When cooking, it's tempting to fall into the habit of thinking that you need a different recipe in order to make changes. Not so. After reading the other chapters in this book, you have a basic knowledge of how ingredients interact. Try making some logically thought-out changes based on that knowledge.

Next, determine what to keep and what to change. Concentrate on making one change at a time. (If you change five things at once, you won't know which one had the desired effect.) Remember that changing often becomes a process of altering suggested methods and exploring new ones. Herein lies the fascination of creating—a process as stimulating in cooking as it is in other forms of art.

Anne's Experimental Cheesecake

Experimenting in the kitchen is something we love to do. On one such bout of experimenting, Anne started with a traditional cheesecake recipe. She thought the flavor of the filling was right, but the base was too sweet. Rather than simply reducing the sugar, she substituted rusk crackers—not sweet, very crisp, a fine crumb when crushed. By subduing the flavor of the crust, the delicate filling could shine.

Cheesecake Experiments

When experimenting in the kitchen, Anne considered a number of possible improvements in a traditional cheese-cake recipe.

Changes that might make the texture more delicate

1. Add air by:
   - whipping the cream
   - beating egg yolks and sugar together well
   - beating egg whites until stiff and folding them in
2. Reduce baking time
3. Change technique
   - folding versus stirring
4. Bake at 325°F (160°C) maximum
5. Wrap base of pan in aluminum foil and bake in a water bath.
6. Remove from oven while center still jiggles slightly
7. Serve cool but not cold

Changes that might improve the appearance

1. Reduce baking time to avoid cracking
2. Run knife around edges as soon as cheesecake is removed from the oven, so the cake doesn't stick to the pan as it contracts
3. Cool away from drafts so the cake cools gradually and evenly

But remember, flavor involves more than just the basic tastes. Anne also felt that the texture of the original dessert was too firm. And invariably the top cracked during baking, something that Anne didn't find aesthetically pleasing. All of the ideas in the sidebar on the left are ones that Anne considered as she thought about how to make the texture more delicate and improve the finished appearance.

If you make changes methodically and keep track of what you're doing, you're following the scientific method.

Eventually, through several trials, Anne developed a recipe that produces a cheesecake that is precisely to her taste.

You've probably made changes in recipes—substituting one ingredient for another, or adding more of a particular spice. You may not think of these changes as scientific experiments, but if you make changes methodically and keep track of what you're doing, you're following the scientific method.

Food at Its Best Blends Art and Science

If you look at cooking objectively, food is both the source of body sustenance and of great delight—its roots lie in science, but the interpretation of the finished dish has much to do with art. And though you may not consciously think of the overlap of these two realms in cooking, it's an integral part of cooking well.

Recently, we enjoyed one of the finest crème brûlées we've ever eaten. Its astoundingly silky custard was topped with a lightly crunchy, still-warm caramelized topping. If you've tried to do this under the broiler of an ordinary oven, you'll know it's hard to achieve a topping that's evenly brown, yet still fragile.

In this dessert, the brûlée was melted using a small propane torch, just before the dessert was served. The torch's extreme heat melted the sugar until it resembled very old, deep amber glass. Our desserts were garnished with three haphazard ringlets of candied tangerine peel, creating intriguing contrasts in flavor and texture.

Making Changes in Baking

You can successfully make changes in recipes for cakes, muffins, cookies, breads, and other baked goods. Here are some tips that will help you along.

• When you are devising something new, use an existing recipe as a guide to establish the ratio of one ingredient to another. For each type of baking, there is a proportion that must be maintained between ingredients that are tenderizers (fat and sugar) and those that are structure builders (flour and eggs). For instance, a standard, plain cake has, by measure, one-third as much fat as sugar; two-thirds as much milk as sugar; and about three times as much flour as liquid.

• You need to measure accurately and keep track of changes so you can repeat your successes—and figure out what went wrong when something is less than successful.

• When you reduce fat and sugar, be aware that you're making a compromise. You'll have fewer calories, yes, but be prepared to sacrifice some tenderness.

• Substituting wholesome grains and specialty flours for all-purpose flour adds nutritional value as well as pizzazz to breads and muffins. The first time you try this, use these flours to replace one-third of the total amount of flour. In successive batches, try increasing the amount to one-half or more. Using some all-purpose flour is worthwhile, as it holds batters and doughs together well and helps support heavier grains.

• You don't always have to change the ingredients to change a recipe. Try using the same ingredients in a different form. For lighter, more airy cakes, don't just add the eggs that the recipe calls for. Instead, try beating the egg yolks with the sugar and the fat until pale and thickened. Then, as a final step, fold beaten egg whites into the batter.

• Baking at the right temperature lets the inside of a batter or dough set before the outside gets too brown. Because a higher sugar content delays setting, there's logic in baking fine cakes and sweet yeast breads at lower temperatures (350–375°F/180–190°C) than leaner batters and doughs (400–425°F/200–220°C).

• Learn to trust your intuition with flavors. Good cooking uses all the senses.

Here was an innovative chef bridging the realms of both art and science to lift a classic to new heights.

We like to think of science as the keystone to how food behaves in cooking. The physical and chemical characteristics of food place parameters on what's possible in the kitchen. But creativity in presentation and skills honed through intuition and practice also deftly play with your senses. In the hands of a good cook, foods stimulate, titillate, tease, and soothe as powerfully as any work of art.

Here was an innovative chef bridging the realms of both art and science to lift a classic to new heights.

And because food involves both art and science, the potential for fresh ideas and new insights is enormous. When cooking successfully bridges both realms, food is elevated beyond the ordinary and the process of making it so becomes ever fascinating. If this book has contributed to your journey toward achieving those aims, we're pleased.

Sources

American Egg Board. *The Egg Handling and Care Guide,* 1990.

The American National Cattlewomen, Inc. *When Is a Steer More Than a Steer?,* 1991.

Andrews, Jean. *Peppers, The Domesticated Capsicums.* Austin, TX: University of Texas Press, 1985.

Atkins, P.W. *Molecules.* (Scientific American Library Series no. 21) New York: W.H. Freeman and Company, 1987.

Auld, Elaine. "Food Editors Prefer 'Umami' Taste Sensation," *Food Insight* (a publication of International Food Information Council), March/April 1992.

Bennion, Marion. *Introductory Foods.* Englewood Cliffs, N.J.: Prentice Hall, 1994.

Beranbaum, Rose Levy. *The Cake Bible.* New York: William Morrow & Company, Inc., 1988.

Boudreau, James C., ed. *Food Taste Chemistry.* Washington, D.C.: American Chemical Society, 1979.

Bowers, Jane. *Food Theory and Applications,* 2d ed. New York: Macmillan Publishing Company, 1992.

Charley, Helen. *Food Science,* 2d ed. New York: John Wiley & Sons, 1982.

Corriher, S. "The Amazing Culinary Powers of Eggs," in *Fine Cooking,* no. 14, April/May 1996.

de Man, John M. *Principles of Food Chemistry.* New York: Van Nostrand Reinhold, 1989.

Freeland-Graves, Jeanne H., and Gladys C. Peckham. *Foundations of Food Preparation,* 6th ed. Englewood Cliffs, N.J.: Prentice Hall, 1996.

Grosser, Arthur E. *The Cookbook Decoder, or Culinary Alchemy Explained.* New York: Warner Books Inc., 1983.

Handbook of Food Preparation. Washington, D.C.: The American Home Economics Association, 1980.

Heath, Henry, and Gary Reineccius. *Flavor Chemistry and Technology.* New York: Van Nostrand Reinhold, 1986.

Hillman, Howard. *Kitchen Science: A Guide to Knowing the Hows and Whys for Fun and Success in the Kitchen.* Boston, MA.: Houghton Mifflin Company, 1981.

International Food Information Council Review on Monosodium Glutamate. *Examining the Myths.* International Food Information Council, 1994.

Maarse, H. *Volatile Compounds in Foods & Beverages.* New York: Marcel Dekker Inc., 1991.

Margen, Sheldon. *Wellness Encyclopedia of Food and Nutrition.* New York: Random House, 1992.

McGee, Harold. *On Food and Cooking: The Science and Lore of the Kitchen.* New York: Collier Books, 1997.

McWilliams, Margaret. *Food Fundamentals.* New York: John Wiley & Sons, 1985.

———. *Foods: Experimental Perspectives.* New York: Macmillan Publishing Company, 1989.

Morton, I.D., and A.J. Macleod, *Food Flavors: Part A. Introduction.* New York: Elsevier Scientific Publishing Company, 1982.

Norman, Jill. *The Complete Book of Spices: A Practical Guide to Spices and Aromatic Seeds.* London: Dorling Kindersley, 1990.

Ortiz, Elisabeth Lambert, ed. *The Encyclopedia of Herbs, Spices and Flavorings: A Cook's Compendium.* London: Dorling Kindersley Limited, 1992.

Pennington, Neil L., and Charles W. Baker. *Sugar: A User's Guide to Sucrose.* New York: Van Nostrand Reinhold, 1990.

Piggott, J. R., and A. Paterson. *Understanding Natural Flavors.* New York: Macmillan Publishing Company, 1994.

Pyler, Ernest J. *Baking Science & Technology,* 3rd ed. Merriam, KS. Sosland Publishing Co., 1988.

Root, Waverly. *Food: An Authoritative and Visual History of the Foods of the World.* New York: Simon & Schuster, Inc., 1980.

Rupp, Rebecca. *Blue Corn and Square Tomatoes: Unusual Facts About Common Vegetables.* Pownal, Vermont: Storey Communications, Inc., 1987.

Schultz, H. W., ed. *Symposium on Foods: The Chemistry and Physiology of Flavors.* Westport, CT: The AVI Publishing Co. Inc., 1967.

Seelig, Tina L. *The Epicurean Laboratory.* New York: W. H. Freeman and Company, 1991.

Self, R. "Potato Flavor," in *Symposium on Foods: The Chemistry and Physiology of Flavors.* Westport, CT: The AVI Publishing Co., Inc., 1967.

U.S. Dept. of Agriculture Food Safety and Inspection Service. *Use a Meat Thermometer & Take the Guesswork Out of Cooking.* (Pamphlet available from USDA, 14th Street & Independence Ave, S.W., Washington, D.C. 20250.)

White, Beverley, ed. *Special Issue on Flavor Perception Trends in Food Science & Technology,* vol. 7, no. 12 (December 1996).

Willan, Anne. *La Varenne Pratique.* London: Dorling Kindersley, 1989.

Index

Acidic foods, 28
  baking soda additions, 57
  sour flavors in, 123
Acidity
  browning of cut fruits
    prevented by, 22
  egg white stability and,
    52
  meat tenderized by, 101
  pH scale, 28
Actinidin, 102
Agar-agar, 107
Air classification, in
  milling, 80, 82
Albumen, 36
Alcohol
  flaming, 2, 135
  as yeast by-product, 61,
    63, 64
Alkaline foods, 28
Alkaloids, 124–125, 127
Alliin/alliinase, 25
Allium, effect of cooking on,
  24–25
All-purpose flour, 81, 82, 94
Almonds, pralined, 74
Amino acids, manufacture
  of by plants, 16
Ammonia, in cooked
  cabbage, 24
Angel food cakes, 45
Anthocyanin pigments, 30
Anthoxanthin pigments, 30
Apples
  air between cells in, 33
  anthocyanin pigments
    in, 30
  cut, browning in, 22
  used with baking soda,
    57
Applesauce, adding sugar
  to, 18
Apprenticeship, learning
  by, 5
Apricots, with baking
  soda, 57

Aroma
  importance of, 129
  pungency and, 126, 128
  sensitivities to, 130
Art, with baker's dough,
  86–87
Artichokes, salted water
  and, 68
Arugula, 16, 17
Ascorbic acid, browning of
  cut fruits prevented by, 22
Asparagus, acidity of, 29
Astringency, 126
Avocados
  bitterness in, 124–125
  cut, browning in, 22
  historical view of, 11

Baker's dough art, 86–87
Baking
  See also Leavening;
    specific baked goods
  making changes in,
    138–139
  role of egg in, 45–46
  role of sugar in, 71–73
Baking powder, 54, 55,
  58–59
  baking soda used with,
    56
Baking soda, 54, 55–58
  acids used with, 55–56,
    57
  baking powder used with,
    56
  pH of, 28, 29
Banana bread, leavening
  for, 59
Bananas
  astringency in, 126
  cut, browning in, 22
  overripe, acidity reduced
    in, 57, 59
  ripening, 19
  storing, 20
  sugars in, 70
  used with baking soda, 57

Barbecued meats, Maillard
  reaction and, 73
Basil, combinations with,
  132–133
Bay laurel, 132, 133
Beans. *See* Green beans;
  Legumes
Bearnaise sauce, 53
Beef, 97–107
  See also Ground beef
  chopped chuck soup, 105
  colors of, 106–107
  cooking temperatures for,
    102
  cuts and cooking meth-
    ods for, 100–102
  ground, 102, 105, 106
  myoglobin in, 106
  nonfood uses of, 99
  searing, 104
  simmering vs. boiling,
    103
  tenderizing, 102–106
  tenderness factors, 97–98,
    100, 101
Beer
  acidity of, 29
  maltose in, 70
  yeast and, 60
Beets
  acidity of, 29
  salted water and, 68
Berries, color of, 30. *See also*
  specific kinds
Betalains, 30
Bitter flavors, 123–125
  astringency and, 126
  temperature and, 125
Blackberries
  seeds, 19
  used with baking soda,
    57
Black pepper, as pungent,
  128
Blanching, browning of cut
  fruits prevented by, 22

Cook's queries
baking soda and baking
powder, 56
folding in egg whites, 50
gooey mashed potatoes,
26
hot peppers, 127
overbeaten egg whites, 51
sauce clarity, 94
sautéing onions
separately, 27
timing poultry cooking,
117
veal tenderness, 104
yeast types, 61
Corn
color stability of, 28
conversion of sugar to
starch in, 22–23
pH of, 29
popping, 33
Cornstarch
in baking powder, 58
as sauce thickener, 94, 95
Corn syrup, freezing egg
yolks with, 40
Cortex of carrot, 14
Crackers, pH of, 29
Cranberries, used with baking soda, 57
Creaming shortening, 92,
94
with sugar, 68, 71
Cream of tartar
in baking powder, 58
in beaten egg white, 52
to prevent yellowing, 30
Creativity, knowledge and,
6–7
Crème caramel/crème
brûlée, 73, 74, 137, 139
Crisper, role of, 15
Cruciferous vegetables. See
Mustard family
Cucumbers
fermentation of, 131
as fruits, 19
storing, 20
Curry, sour flavors and, 123
Custard
chalazae and, 35

cooking temperature and,
43, 44

Dates, phenols and color of,
22
Disaccharides, food sources
of, 70
Disappearance data, sugar
and, 69, 71
Dough, gluten in, 78–80
Dough art, 86–87

Egg beaters, 51
Eggplant
as fruits, 19
storing, 20
Eggs, 34–53
See also Egg whites;
Egg yolks
anatomy of, 35–37
binding role of, 44–46
boiling tips, 40–42
cooking time and tender-
ness of, 38
as emulsions, 52, 53
freezing, 40
freshness concerns,
37–39, 49, 51
frying, 43
gentle vs. high heat and,
43
hard-cooked, 38, 41
as leavening, 45, 46
in piecrust, 83
poached, 37–38
proteins, 35
raw vs. hard-cooked, 41
separating, 39
shell color, 37
soft-cooking, 41–42
using at room tempera-
ture, 39
Egg whites, 36, 47–52
as alkaline, 28
beaten, stages of, 47–49
clarifying broth with, 53
"folding in," 50
overbeaten, salvaging, 51
salt and, 66
storing, 40

sugar and, 48, 51–52
warming, 39
Egg yolks, 36, 37
contamination of whites
by, 49, 51
in emulsions, 52, 53
storing, 40
Elasticity, gluten and, 80
Emulsifiers, gluten and, 94
Emulsions, egg yolks in, 52,
53
Endosperm
in flour, 80
in wheat kernel, 78
Ethylene-ripened vs. home-
grown tomatoes, 8
Eugenol, as vanillin source,
124
Experimentation, learning
by, 2
Experiments
applesauce, 18
cheesecake, 2, 135–137
chopping chuck for soup,
105
egg protein and heat, 43
mixing muffin batter, 90
roasting garlic, 25
roasting vs. boiling, 128

Fat
See also Shortening
in fish, 109
meat tenderness and,
97–98
in muffin batter, 91
as tenderizer, 88–89, 94
Fermentation
flavors developed by, 131
yeast's role in, 60, 63–64
Figs, phenols and color of,
22
Fish, 108–113
cooking methods for,
111–112
cooking times for, 110,
111, 112
fat vs. lean, 109
freshness factors, 109–110
frozen, 110
marinades for, 112–113

Salad greens (*continued*)
storing, 16–18
Salt, 64–69
for baker's dough art, 87
delaying addition of, 66
in egg-poaching water,
38
freezing egg yolks with,
40
in ice cream making, 67
in pasta or vegetable
water, 68
"pinch" of, 66
as preservative, 66
sources of, 64–65, 66
Salty flavors, 122–123
temperature and, 125
Sauces
adding salt to, 66
thickeners for, 94, 95
Sauerkraut, as fermentation
product, 131
Savory, combinations with,
133
Science, cooking and, 7–9
Sea salt, 65
Seasonings, using, 132–133
Sea water, pH of, 29
Seeds, 22–23
Shortening
creaming, 92, 94
creaming sugar and, 68,
71
pastry tenderness and,
88–89
Simmering vs. boiling meat,
103
Smell, sense of, 130. *See also*
Aromas
Snap beans. *See* Green
beans
Sodium bicarbonate. *See*
Baking soda
Sodium chloride. *See* Salt
Soil nutrients, legumes and,
32
Soufflé, beating egg whites
for, 47–49
Sour cream, used with
baking soda, 56, 57

Sour flavors, 123
Sour milk, used with baking
soda, 56
Soy sauce, as fermentation
product, 131
Spices
dry roasting and flavor
of, 131
sources of, 133
using, 132, 133
Spinach
acidity of, 29
salted water and, 68
Squash, as fruit, 19
Squash, winter
acidity of, 29
color stability of, 28
effect of baking on, 26
storing, 20
Starch, in flour, 80. *See also*
Cornstarch
Steam
in baking bread, 64
popovers and, 46
Steaming fish, 112
Stewing
apples, poaching vs., 18
meat, temperature for,
103
Stir-frying
color of vegetables and,
28
preparing meat for, 105
Stock, adding salt to, 66
Storage. *See specific foods*
Strawberries, acidity of, 29
Sucrose, sources of, 70, 71
Sugar, 69–75
adding to applesauce, 18
in beaten egg white, 48,
51–52
browning and, 72–73
browning of cut fruits
prevented by, 22
caramelizing, 73, 74
consumption of, 69, 71
creaming shortening
with, 68, 71
as flavor enhancer,
121–122

food sources of, 70
freezing and, 72
freezing egg yolks with,
40
in jams or jellies, 75
role of in baking, 71–73
as tenderizer, 71–72, 94
yeast activated by, 61, 63
Sulfate, in baking powder,
59
Sulfur-containing com-
pounds, in cut onions, 31
Suspicions about foods, 11
Sweet potatoes
acidity of, 29
color stability of, 28
roasting vs. boiling, 128
storing, 20
Sweet tastes, 121–122, 125
Symbiosis, 32
Syrup, sugar, 73, 75

Table salt, 65. *See also* Salt
Tannins, astringency and,
126
Taproots, 12–13
Tarragon, combinations
with, 132–133
Taste sensations, 125–128
astringency, 126
pungency, 126, 128
temperature and, 125
texture and, 125–126
Tastes. *See* Flavors
T-bone steak, marbling in,
98
Tea
astringency in, 126
bitterness in, 124
Television cooking shows,
as learning source, 6
Temperature of foods
flavor changes and, 131
taste and, 125
Tenderizer, sugar as, 71–72
Tenderizing meats, 101–106
Tenderness of meats, 97–98,
100, 101
Texture, flavor and,
125–126

Credits and Acknowledgments

Edited at the Exploratorium by Pat Murphy
Design by Gary Crounse
Illustration by Esther Kutnick
Production editing by Ellyn Hament
Design production by Stacey Luce

Image Credits

All illustrations by Esther Kutnick.
Page 14: Jennifer Johnson and Kent McDonald; page 20: image based on data published by J. Y. Do, D. K. Slaunkhe, and L. E. Olson in *Journal of Food Science,* 1969; page 33: Jennifer Lonsdale and Paula Sicurello; page 49: Joan Venticinque; page 60: copyright David Scharf/Peter Arnold, Inc.; page 66: courtesy of Cargill Salt; pages 68 and 79: courtesy of Philips ElectroScan; pages 86 and 87: Pani & Fili, Breads & Threads of Italy, Vima de Marchi Micheli, Curator; page 95: courtesy of National Starch and Chemical Company; page 150: Al Harvey.

Acknowledgments from the Exploratorium

At the Exploratorium, no one works alone. This book would not exist without the efforts of many members of the Exploratorium staff and friends of the Exploratorium.

Thanks to Gary Crounse for his design work and pataphysical serenity in moments of panic; to Esther Kutnick for her fine illustrations; to Megan Bury for her photo research and assistance with all the squirrelly details; to Stacey Luce for her production work and smiling acceptance in times of crisis; to Ellen Klages for her meticulous copyediting; to Ellyn Hament for her valiant efforts to catch every last error; to Larry Antila for his courier services; to Ruth Brown for her (as always) sage advice; to Kurt Feichtmeir for his cheerful support and budgeting acumen; to Rob Semper for his continuing support of our publishing enterprise; and to our scientific advisors, Charles Carlson and Karen Kalumuck, for reviewing the manuscript from the biological perspective. Special thanks to David Sobel at Henry Holt and Company for his editing expertise.

And of course, I'd like to thank our authors, the ever-inquisitive Anne and Sue, who encouraged me to attempt crème brûlée—and, with the help of science, to succeed!

—Pat Murphy

About the Authors

Since 1983, sisters Anne Gardiner (right) and Sue Wilson (left) have been partners in The Inquisitive Cook, an enterprise that focuses on the science that lies behind cooking. About their work, they write: "We're never sure whether we should cast ourselves as writers who teach, or teachers who write."

Clearly, they are both. They've taught classes on the chemistry of cooking through the Continuing Education Department at the University of British Columbia and at numerous cooking schools. Currently, they are teaching food theory in the School of Family and Nutritional Sciences at the University of British Columbia. They have enjoyed sharing their perspective on food as guest speakers who can take the mystery out of cooking.

Since 1988, they have also written magazine articles and a weekly column titled "The Inquisitive Cook," which appears in Canadian newspapers.

You can visit Anne and Sue's award-winning Web site at: http://www.inquisitivecook.com

About the Exploratorium

The Exploratorium, San Francisco's museum of science, art, and human perception, is a place where people of all ages make discoveries about the world around them. The museum has over 600 exhibits, and all of them run on curiosity. You don't just look at these exhibits—you experiment with them. At the Exploratorium's exhibits, you can play with a captive tornado, generate an electric current, see what's inside a cow's eye, and investigate hundreds of fascinating natural phenomena.

Each year, over half a million people visit the museum. Through programs for teachers, the Exploratorium also encourages students to learn by asking their own questions and experimenting to find the answers. Through publications like this one, the Exploratorium brings the excitement of learning by doing to people everywhere.

Visit the Exploratorium's home page on the World Wide Web at:

http://www.exploratorium.edu

Next time you are in San Francisco, come visit the Exploratorium!

San Francisco

EXPLORaTORiUM

**The Museum of Science, Art,
and Human Perception**